G000019224

Prime Time

Communication and Language

An active approach to developing communication skills

Jo Blank and Alice Bevan

Contents

Published by Practical Pre-School Books, A Division of MA Education Ltd, St Jude's Church, Dulwich Road, Herne Hill, London, SE24 0PB.
Tel: 020 7738 5454 www.practicalpreschoolbooks.com

Associate Publisher: Angela Morano Shaw

Design: Alison Coombes **fonthill**creative 01722 717043

© MA Education Ltd 2017. All photos copyright MA Education Ltd.

Introduction

The national picture

'Language is THE fundamental life skill.' (I CAN, 2016)

'Good communication and language skills are vital for children's life chances.' (Nash, Lowe, Leah, 2013)

By the time children start school, it is expected that they are relatively competent communicators. It is anticipated that they are able to *'understand much of what is said, express themselves clearly, share their feelings and make their needs known.'* (I CAN, 2008). However, more and more often children are not meeting this expectation.

Research shows that a growing number of young children in the UK start school with communication and language needs. The Communication Trust (2013) estimates that around 10% of children have a speech, language or communication difficulty. They also report that in some parts of the UK, particularly in areas of deprivation, over 50% of children start school with speech, language and communication needs. This means that thousands of children are starting school each year without the language that they need for learning. It also means that there are children with communication difficulties in most early years settings.

Children's experiences at home

Children learn to communicate through interactions with those close to them, therefore *'language is affected by home patterns of communication.'* (Dickinson et al, 2012). This refers to both the quality and amount of language spoken in the home.

The National Literacy Trust released research findings in 2011 which showed that:
- 20% of new parents are unaware of the need to communicate with their young baby
- 19% of parents believe it is only beneficial to communicate with babies from the age of three months
- 6% of parents believe that communicating with their baby is only necessary when they are six months or older
- 13% of parents believe that the primary responsibility for developing their child's communication skills lies outside the home.

This leads us to believe that over 25% of children do not have sufficient language interaction at home to guarantee healthy and normal development of their communication and language skills.

'A child's experiences from birth to five have a major impact on their future life chances' (EYFS Framework DfE, 2014). This is well illustrated by the I CAN Impact Report (2016),

'A child's vocabulary at age 5 is recognised as being a strong predictor of literacy abilities, mental health and employment status later in life.'

This speaks volumes for the role of the early years educator in promoting these critical skills. Communication and language is one of the three prime areas of learning and development in the EYFS Framework (2017). Along with Physical development and Personal social and emotional development, it underpins all other learning. These three areas 'are particularly crucial for igniting children's curiosity and enthusiasm for learning, and for building their capacity to learn, form relationships and thrive'.

Children's experience of technology

Strong links have been made between the use of TV and other electronic devices and children's communication and language delay. With the growing use of mobile phones and tablets, children are growing up in a world where communication takes place more so on a screen rather than face to face with people in a real space.

Several recent studies suggest that increased exposure to technology could be having a negative impact on attention development in children. Evans Schmidt et al (in Spooner and Woodcock, 2010) found that background television significantly affected children's attention to play, even when they appeared not to be watching it.

The impact of poor language and communication skills

Evidence and research from the Communication Trust between 2009 and 2016 reveals that the impact of language difficulty on children's lives can be devastating.

1. **In school:** Children who start school with communication difficulties are at a great disadvantage, because they are likely to struggle to understand what the staff and other children are saying, and have difficulty expressing their basic needs and feelings. They are likely to experience:
   - **Literacy and numeracy difficulties**
     Children with poor early language at age five are four times more likely to struggle with reading at age 11. Between 50-90% of children with persistent speech, language and communication difficulties go on to experience reading difficulties.
   - **Social isolation**
     Social play is about communicating thoughts and

ideas to others, which with young children can be through actions, expressions and body language. However, as children mature, their play becomes more dependent on spoken language to share ideas. It follows that children without these skills find it hard to join in and are likely to be left out of group play.
   - **Low self-esteem**
     Young people with language difficulties are three times more likely to have mental health issues. Being aware of your own limitations in any aspect of life skills when everyone around you appears competent, can lead to a feeling of hopelessness, inadequacy and consequently a poor self-image.
   - **Challenging behaviour**
     Two thirds of children aged 7 -14 years with serious behaviour problems also have language difficulties.

2. **Throughout life:** If these problems are not resolved, it is disturbing to learn that people with language and communication difficulties are at greater risk of:
   - **Unemployment**
     More than 8 out of 10 long-term unemployed young men have been found to have speech, language and communication needs
   - **Mental Health issues**
     Young people with language difficulties are three times more likely to have mental health issues
   - **Committing crime**
     Between 60 and 90% of young offenders have speech, language and communication needs.

About this book

The central theme in this book is how children can be helped to communicate and to use language through an **active** approach. This is primarily about a **physically active approach**, which is part of an overall **active learning approach**. Young children learn well through being physical, since being physical is an inbuilt urge for them. There is also a huge emphasis on the crucial role of **interaction** between adults and children and children themselves in order for communication and language to develop.

Why is the emphasis on learning through an ACTIVE approach?

An **active learning** approach is a 'first-hand experience and hands-on' approach. It means children are actively involved in their learning. In their play they handle objects, use all their senses to find out what the objects can do and how they work; they use objects in ways that are meaningful for them and they make mistakes. For example, only by repeatedly trying to put a large block inside a small container do they learn about size.

Only by holding a ball, feeling its roundness, letting it go and watching it as it rolls do children learn that balls roll. All of this takes time and children have to have these experiences for themselves to construct their own knowledge and understanding. All of this learning is enhanced and facilitated through the support and INTERACTION of other children and adults.

> *'Active learning is defined as learning in which the child, by acting on objects and interacting with people, ideas, and events, constructs new understanding. No one else can have experiences for the child or construct knowledge for the child. Children must do this for themselves.'*
> (Hohmann and Weikart, 1995)

The key to understanding something and learning is for it to be meaningful to the learner. This means that the new learning has to connect to what we already know to make sense to us. How we learn something impacts on whether we can make those connections. As adults, we know that it is easier to learn things if we are interested in them. It is also helpful to engage with the task and take an active part in it.

For children, the Statutory Framework for the EYFS (2017) does a great job in explaining the characteristics of effective learning, and how children learn best through play and exploration, being actively engaged and being able to have their own ideas and think critically about things. These ways of learning all require an active involvement in the process, and communication is an integral part of that process. To take this a stage further and make the 'active' involvement a physical one is a matter of tuning in to children's natural urge to move. It is also a belief that by 'doing', things become more meaningful. Also, if there is an element of emotion such as enjoyment attached to what we do, we are more likely to remember it.

Jensen (2005) has drawn together research to support this and tells us that physical activity affects learning ability. As the blood flows to the brain the oxygen and nutrient supplies are increased. This affects the working of our neurotransmitters (the chemicals in our brain that transmit information throughout our brain and body) and this has a positive effect on our mood and our memory. This means that impressions that are absorbed through a variety of senses, such as hearing, sight and the felt sense of body are memorized for a longer period of time. This is strong evidence that movement really aids learning. (Strick 1994, in Jensen, 2005).

Jensen (2005) highlights various studies that support the relationship between movement and the workings of the brain; there are links between movement and the visual system (Shulman et al., 1997), movement and the language systems (Kim, Ugirbil, & Strick, 1994), movement and memory (Desmond, Gabrielli, Wagner, Ginier, & Glover, 1997), and movement and attention (Courchesne & Allen, 1997).

There is a significant link between the vestibular system (sense of balance located in the inner ear), the cerebellum (the centre for motor control) and the cortex (the thinking part of the brain). The interaction between these areas helps us keep our balance, turn thoughts into actions, and coordinate movements. That is why activities that stimulate inner-ear motion, like swinging, rolling, and jumping are really valuable for cognitive development. Palmer (in Jensen, 2005) found children made significant gains in attention and reading from this type of vestibular activity.

The main purpose of Prime Time Communication and Language is to help children to communicate well, in a variety of ways and to become confident talkers. We promote active learning and mainly physically active experiences as the key way to do this, based on research outlined above.

As humans, we communicate in a wide variety of ways, for example, through body language, facial expressions, spoken language and sign language. Learning anything involves using our senses, of sight, hearing, touch, taste and smell. Learning is often a physical experience. Children learn about themselves through bodily actions and sensory feelings, by discovering what their bodies can do, and how they can physically interact with the world around them.

The 5 main sections of the book cover key aspects of communication and language and are based around the Communication Pyramid. This has a variety of sources, one of these being the Royal College of Speech and Language Therapists (2012). We have created a climbing frame to represent the Pyramid, to emphasise the physical theme throughout the book. This is referred to as the '**Communication Climbing Frame**'.

Communication Climbing Frame

The Communication Climbing Frame embraces the vital elements of communication and language. In order to be a successful communicator, children need to acquire a certain level of competence in all of the five areas. For example, before a child is able to talk in sentences and communicate effectively, they must acquire skills in attention and listening, social communication and understanding. Although children may often develop these skills simultaneously, it is helpful to consider each area individually in order to help children with their specific development and to pinpoint difficulties. Each area depends on the others for success; they are totally interlinked.

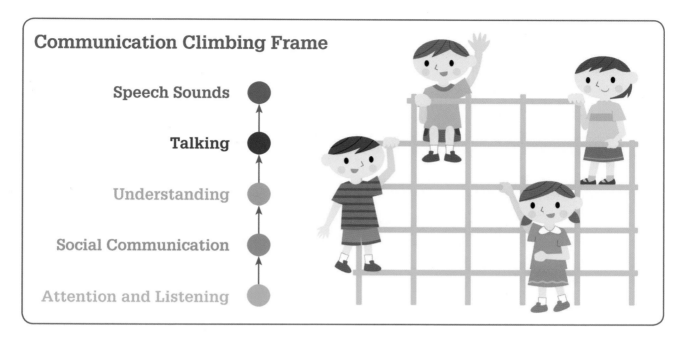

Everyday we communicate with a range of different people for different reasons. Although it may seem simple, communication is in fact a very complex process. Communicating successfully with someone else involves '*a chain of interlinked processes that enables us to understand and convey messages.*' (Elks and McLachlan, 2015).

The Communication Chain (Elks and McLachlan, 2015) shows the process of communication; what happens, step by step in our heads when we communicate with others.

Fully understanding what someone else is saying requires a range of processes including paying attention to them and interpreting non-verbal communication. It also involves being able to hear, listening to what they are saying, and remembering these words in order to process and understand them.

As well as simply being able to understand the single words, you, of course, must be able to understand all the sentences used and then interpret the meaning of what has been said.

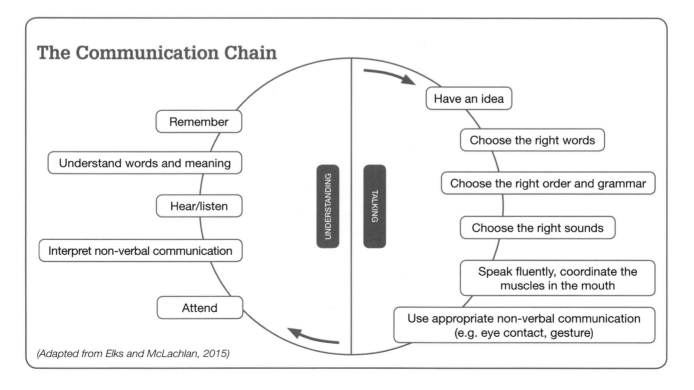

(Adapted from Elks and McLachlan, 2015)

The act of talking requires you to have an idea that you want to communicate in the first place. Before this message comes out of your mouth, you need to choose the words and plan how these words go together. This process happens so quickly, that it is easy to forget how complex the process actually is. You then need to select the sounds that make up the words you are going to use and then say these sound combinations fluently. When the verbal message is spoken, this is accompanied with non-verbal communication.

As highlighted already, many children reach the end of the Early Years Foundation Stage with communication difficulties. If a child has difficulties with one area in the **communication chain**, this usually has an impact on other aspects of the chain, which makes successful communication a challenge.

Each section in this book refers back to this **communication chain**, to help you consider the bigger picture when learning about the five key areas shown on the **Communication Climbing Frame**.

The key feature that underpins the development of all these aspects of communication is **interaction, the interaction between the adult and the child, and between children themselves**.

There are also **Tables of development** at the end of each section to help you check your children's stage and progress.

'**The adult role**' part of each section of the book, (based on the **Communication Climbing Frame**), includes guidance on:
- an active approach
- play and interaction
- a communication-rich environment
- crucial links with parents
- children for whom English is not their first language (EAL)
- children with specific communication and language difficulties.

The aim of the 8-week programme is to embed an active approach to developing children's communication and language skills. An overall physically active and 'active learning' approach will enrich the overall ethos and learning climate in your setting. It takes you, the practitioner, through a step by step developmental process to increase your knowledge and understanding, and build up a strong communication-friendly environment. The programme focuses on developing the quality of interactions between staff and children, and children themselves. It provides a wide range of physical and active learning activities to foster children's competence in communication and language.

Interaction is the key

As early years practitioners, we are entrusted to care for and educate babies and young children. This means helping each one to become a unique person with individual talents, able to enjoy life experiences and function successfully within our society. It is through building trusting relationships and having meaningful, perceptive interactions that we are able to aspire to this tall order and hugely important role.

The way we develop relationships is through interactions; the way we interact is through communication and language. How we, as practitioners, communicate and use language is therefore key to how well children learn and develop in all areas, including communication and language. We are highly influential role models in their lives.

Children unconsciously mirror or imitate what they see in their environment, which includes the practitioner. For example, we see babies who are a few days old stick out their tongue to copy the adult. We have what are called 'mirror neurons' in our brain that have been found to help in the development of language, empathy and play (Rizzolatti et al, 1995, 2002; Meltzoff and Prinz, 2002; Lacoboni, 2008; in Robinson 2011). Children will mirror the practitioner's emotions, actions and how they communicate.

As a significant role model, and to have a positive impact, you (the practitioner), must pay attention to your language, body language, behaviour and feelings when with the children.

> *"Children are like wet cement. Whatever falls on them makes an impression"*
> (Haim Ginott, 2016)

Principles for good practice

These principles defined by Dickinson et al, (2012), cover key ways for adults to promote good communication and language skills through their everyday interactions with children.

Principle 1: Children need to hear many words often
Principle 2: Children learn words when they are interested
Principle 3: Children learn best when adults are responsive to them
Principle 4: Words are learned when meanings are made clear
Principle 5: Vocabulary and grammar are learned together
Principle 6: Keep it positive

Each section of the book refers to how these principles support best practice.

A communication friendly environment

'We are all consciously and subconsciously affected by our environment. It can affect our thoughts, feelings and behaviours'. (Jarman, 2009)

The nature of the environment is a crucial factor in encouraging interaction between adults and children and the children themselves. Elizabeth Jarman (2006) developed an approach to setting up the whole environment where speaking and listening skills, emotional well-being, physical development and general engagement are central to how it is organised. She looks at how noise, colour, light and storage, affect communication and social interactions and how resources can be used creatively to appeal to individual children and so trigger talking. She considers *'softness and homeliness, open-ended resources, seasonal resources, recycled and re-purposed materials, according to children's fascinations.'* In each section for '**The adult role**' we look at ways to enhance your environment to nurture each of the specific communication and language skills. It is about setting up 'Communication Friendly Spaces' indoors and outdoors, where children are motivated to chat and feel comfortable.

Children learning English as an Additional Language (EAL)

EAL refers to **English as an additional language**. EAL learners are those who are exposed to a language that is not English at home.

'There are increasing numbers of children entering Early Years Foundation Stage (EYFS) settings for whom English is not the dominant language in the home.' (Department for children, schools and families, 2007)

As more children who are learning EAL are entering early years settings, it is vitally important that you feel confident in how best to support these children.

In this book, EAL features in each section under '**The adult role**' and provides guidance on how best to help these children with that particular aspect of their communication and language development.

'Children learning EAL have the potential to become high-achieving and successful lifelong learners.' (Sargent, 2016)

The way you interact with the children varies according to the child's experience of hearing and speaking English and their understanding and experience of British customs. Some children in your setting will be hearing English for the first time when they enter your setting. Other children will have heard it from birth or a very young age and may be fairly competent at using English as well as another language, even though English may not be their first language.

British customs

Children's experience of British customs is important because it affects the way they interact socially with adults and other children. Children's own social cultural ways influence how they interact with others. For example, in many Asian cultures, they do not expect eye contact because it can appear hostile or rude. The Chinese look at the ground when they greet you as a mark of respect; in Japan, it is inappropriate to smile at strangers. In some cultures it is usual to talk loudly, shout over people, not to wait in a queue (so children are not used to turn taking) and some children may not be used to adults playing with them.

'Social communication behaviors such as eye contact, facial expressions, and body language, are influenced by sociocultural and individual factors.' (www.asha.org)

The Importance of the home language

It is important that parents continue to speak the child's first language at home because the first language:
- is an important part of the child's identity
- significantly helps with learning other languages
- helps the child understand about using language
(Department for children, schools and families, 2007)

Children will learn English at different rates. Some children go through an extended period of silence when entering an unfamiliar language environment; others continue to speak their home language for longer in an attempt to communicate.

See '**The adult role**' in each section for further guidance on children learning EAL.

Section 1: Active Attention and Listening

Why is it important?

- Speech Sounds
- Talking
- Understanding
- Social Communication
- **Attention and Listening**

'The abilities to attend, to listen and to look are prerequisites for all forms of learning, including learning communication, speech and language.'
(Garforth, 2009)

This section is all about the development of attention and listening skills and explains how they impact on every area of communication. They are often described as the building blocks of communication development and form the foundation for all the other communication skills.

The **Communication Climbing Frame** shows attention and listening skills at the base, which means that they support the rest of the language and communication skills. None of the others can be mastered unless children attend to people, things and actions.

Take a look at the **Communication Chain** (page 5) and you will see that to attend, hear and listen come right at the start. So these skills are fundamental to language development.

'Many children presenting with early language delay have been found to have immature attention control, and remedial work on attention problems has helped the children to develop language.' (Reynell, 1980)

> **Early Learning Goal (expected achievement for children by the end of the EYFS)**
>
> **Listening and attention:** children listen attentively in a range of situations. They listen to stories, accurately anticipating key events and respond to what they hear with relevant comments, questions or actions. They give their attention to what others say and respond appropriately, while engaged in another activity. (Statutory Framework for the EYFS, 2017)

To pay attention to something is to concentrate, to focus and to keep your mind on something. Concentration is a fundamental feature of learning and so also underpins the development of communication and language. Listening requires paying attention to something, for example, a child sharing a story book with an adult needs to be able to follow the pictures in the book. Being able to concentrate therefore precedes listening skills.

Children learn through what they see, hear and do. To learn language and how to communicate with others, they have to pay attention to people, objects and tasks. The ability to focus and to maintain attention is therefore vital in learning language.

Babies are exposed to many sounds over their first year and are 'tuning in' to the specific sounds of their mother tongue. Time talking and singing with babies, holds their attention and gives them chance to assimilate the sounds and music of their home language. Giving a 'running commentary' and pointing to things draws their attention to things in the environment and is essential for their healthy development in language and communication.

What is attention?

> 'Attention is the ability to 'selectively focus our attention on specific features of our environment.' (Ward, 2004)

It is important to look at how young children develop their ability to focus and concentrate on people things, and activities, because in order to focus on listening and language children need to concentrate. Let's explore attention skills generally, looking at children's concentration as they play, and how children develop these skills over time. This spans from the often fleeting attention of babies to the intensive concentration of the 4 year old who is determined to build a pirate ship. Children gradually develop the ability to focus on a task for longer periods of time, they then learn to switch their focus of attention from one object or activity to another. Following this, children learn to listen while carrying out a task at the same time.

By the time a child is five years old, they will typically have gone through five stages of attention development (Cooper, Moodley and Reynell, 1978). These can be seen in Tables of development (page 25).

Fleeting attention (0-1 year)
Rigid attention (1-2 years)
Single-chanelled attention (2-3 years)
Focusing attention (3-4 years)
Two-chanelled attention (4-5 years)
(age bands are approximate)

Here are some examples that demonstrate children's attention span.

Case study: Charlie, 3 years 2 months
Charlie plays with toys he chooses himself for 10 minutes and can complete activities such as puzzles. Sometimes he will stop what he is doing to listen if an adult talks to him while he is playing.

During group time at nursery, Charlie usually looks towards the nursery staff when they are talking, he enjoys listening to stories and joining in action songs. He responds appropriately to group instructions most of the time, for example, he will stand up when the adult says 'everyone stand up'.

Charlie's attention and listening skills are typical for his age.

Case study: Laszlo, 3 years 2 months PART 1

Laszlo moves very quickly from one activity to another in the nursery, he flits about and finds it difficult to complete an activity. Laszlo doesn't always respond when the nursery staff call his name.

During group time Laszlo is distracted by any noises he hears and any movements he sees. The nursery staff often have to repeat things several times and get him to 'listen' by getting down to eye-level and speaking directly to him with good eye contact.

When with his key person, Sam, Laszlo can focus for longer, especially if this is in a quiet place.

Laszlo looks towards the practitioner more at group time when they use puppets and story-telling aids. He joins in the actions for the songs.

Laszlo's attention and listening skills are delayed for his age.

There is more information about the steps that staff have taken to support Laszlo with his attention and listening skills. **(See Case study: Laszlo PART 2, page 17)**

Attention, well-being and involvement

Being able to pay attention and focus on something is dependent on many factors. Ferre Laevers (2009) identified a wide range of reasons affecting children's involvement in their activity. How a child feels significantly affects their ability to concentrate. Laevers (2009) developed 5-point scales for both well-being and involvement that, when evaluated, indicate the depth of learning taking place. Well-being is about feeling at ease, being spontaneous and free of emotional tensions, feeling self-confident, good about yourself and being resilient. Involvement refers to the degree of engagement in activities, and intense involvement denotes deep level learning and development.

Below is a summary of the scales adapted from http://www.magicnursery.co.uk/pdf_documents/LevelsofWellBeing.pdf It is suggested that practitioners observe the children individually or as a group for about 2 minutes, then give a score for well-being and/or involvement using the 5-point scale. Learning will be limited during scales 1-3, and children will not be expected to be operating at levels 4 or 5 all of the time. Levels will fluctuate throughout the day.

Heuristic Play

Heuristic play is a powerful way to promote not only long spells of involvement and attention, but to strongly develop children's thinking powers. This term originates from the Greek word 'eurisko' which means 'I discover' and is linked to 'Eureka', a saying made famous by Archimedes in his bath, meaning 'I understand'. So, here lies the essence of heuristic play, which was developed by Elinor Goldschmied and introduced in her book 'People Under Three' (1994). It is about discovery and finding out, using a wide range of natural materials, and recycled household objects in different ways. It is play where babies and toddlers explore natural materials, and play with them in any way they wish without adult intervention. They use their senses to explore the properties of things and what happens if they are rolled, banged, squeezed, moved, joined together, and tasted. It is the type of play that fascinates babies, toddlers and young children and fosters serious concentration. (See **Get Active!** for ideas for Treasure baskets and Heuristic play for toddlers).

The Leuven Scale for well-being

Level	Well-being	Signals
1	Extremely low	The child shows signs of discomfort such as crying or screaming. They may look dejected, sad, frightened or angry. The child does not respond to the environment, avoids contact and is withdrawn. The child may behave aggressively, hurting him/herself or others.
2	Low	The posture, facial expression and actions indicate that the child does not feel at ease. However, the signals are less explicit than under level 1 or the sense of discomfort is not expressed the whole time.
3	Moderate	The child has a neutral posture. Facial expression and posture show little or no emotion. There are no signs indicating sadness or pleasure, comfort or discomfort.
4	High	The child shows obvious signs of satisfaction (as listed under level 5). However, these signals are not constantly present with the same intensity.
5	Extremely High	The child looks happy and cheerful, smiles, cries out with pleasure. They may be lively and full of energy. Actions can be spontaneous and expressive. The child may talk to him/herself, play with sounds, hum or sing. The child appears relaxed and does not show any signs of stress or tension. They can easily access the environment. The child expresses self-confidence and self-assurance.

The Leuven Scale for involvement

Level	Involvement	Signals
1	Extremely Low	Their activity is simple, repetitive and passive. The child seems absent and displays no energy. They may stare into space or look around to see what others are doing.
2	Low	Their activity is spasmodic. The child will be engaged in the activity for some of the time, but there will be moments of non-activity when they will stare into space, or be distracted by what is going on around them.
3	Moderate	Their activity is mainly continuous. The child takes part in the activity but at a fairly routine level and there are few signs of real involvement. They make some progress with what they are doing but don't show much energy and concentration and can be easily distracted.
4	High	They are continually involved in the activity and there are some intense moments. They are not easily distracted.
5	Extremely High	The child shows continuous and intense activity revealing the greatest involvement. They are concentrated, creative, energetic and persistent throughout nearly all the observed period.

What is listening?

Listening can be defined as to *'give one's attention to a sound'* (Oxford Dictionary of English, 2006). Therefore listening refers to the ability to focus on a sound and the attempt to interpret what has been heard. It is important to remember that listening and hearing are not the same thing.

Hearing is defined as the ability *'to perceive with the ear the sound (made by someone or something)'* (Oxford Dictionary of English, 2006).

In order to **listen**, a child must be able to **hear**. However, a child can have perfect hearing, but have great difficulties with listening, particularly if they have attention difficulties. Can you think of a time where you have heard someone talking but not really listened to what they were saying? You might have been thinking about something else, you could hear them talking, but you weren't actually listening and paying attention to what they were saying.

Children learn so much through what they hear as well as through what they see and do. Children who have good attention skills will find it easier to listen, and therefore will learn more easily from what they hear.

Listening requires attention, concentration and focus and this is how we learn spoken language.

'Learning to listen to the target language improves language ability.' (Renukadevi, 2014)

The impact of technology

Several recent studies suggest that increased exposure to technology could be having a negative impact on attention development in children. Even background TV affects children's attention to play. An extensive television diet has long been a concern for parents and teachers.

'A recent study concluded that 'for every extra hour of television (per day) watched as a pre-schooler, the children had 10% additional risk of developing attention difficulties.' (Spooner and Woodcock, 2013)

With the huge presence of technology within most family homes, in terms of TV, computers, iPads and mobile phones, it is vital that early years settings are promoting language and communication skills as much as possible.

The adult role

'By facilitating children's attention and listening skills, we are able to give them a better chance of achieving their potential in communication, speech and language, and therefore learning skills.' (Garforth, 2009)

1. Take an active approach

Use the natural world as a stimulus for learning. Children's attention can be captured and held by movement, either by watching or trying to imitate. Imagine watching a gymnast or a dancer; we are captivated by their skill and fluidity. For a child, an animal, caterpillar, butterfly, insect or bird may catch their attention. The wonders of nature and the movement will fascinate them. Children will become absorbed with the properties of natural materials and how they behave when mixed together, such as water, sand and soil. Fascination leads to a prolonged attention span.

Do lots of action rhymes. When singing action rhymes, it is the movements that children learn first, long before the words. They find it more interesting and meaningful to watch and match movements to words. Their attention will be held by trying to copy the movements. They also love moving their bodies in different ways and in rhythm.

Match movement to words to help children understand them. Simply doing the actions for 'up' and 'down' creates understanding. Prepositions such as under, through or inside are easily understood when squirming through tunnels and negotiating the climbing equipment. Comment on children's movements, 'you are inside the box!' and say things like 'Teddy is under the blanket', or 'behind the cushion' to make these words visually meaningful. It encourages children to 'look' as well as 'listen', which naturally prompts and holds attention for longer. Telling a story using puppets and moving them to do things will quickly capture attention.

Children are naturally active little beings! Give them instructions to run, jump, or throw a bean bag and they are likely to listen!

Help children to be actively involved in their learning, so that they feel in control, excited, and consequently highly motivated. Encourage them to add and find resources to extend their play, to talk about their ideas and share them with others, and to reflect on what they are doing so that they can change things for the better.

So, using an active approach to developing young children's attention and listening skills is a winning strategy every time. It is the most natural way to gain and hold children's attention and enable them to listen and learn.

2. Play and Interact

As a key person, you have a vital role to play in developing children's attention and listening skills. As the person who spends the most time with the baby, toddler or young child, you can nurture concentration through everyday conversations and having fun with them. The baby has fewer voices to assimilate, which helps with 'tuning in' to language sounds. Find out what really interests your children and use this to captivate their attention.

When playing and interacting with the children in your setting, there are some simple strategies that you can use to support their attention and listening skills.

- **Say the child's name** and ensure you have their attention before speaking to them.

- **Physically get down to the same level** as the children so that you are at the same eye level. This will make it easier for them to look at you when you are talking, and easier for them to listen.

- **Be enthusiastic!** Make your voice sound interesting. Use plenty of intonation and use exaggerated facial expressions to keep the children engaged, for example use different voices during story time. Use puppets and toys to tell stories.
(Principle 2: Children learn words when they are interested)

- **Keep your language simple, clear, consistent and relevant**. Meaningful language that links to what they are doing and what they can see, with sensitive repetition is more likely to hold their attention.
(Principle 1: Children need to hear many words often)

- **Use lots of non-verbal communication**, such as gestures and pointing to accompany what you are saying to the children.

- **Be realistic in your expectations** for how long children should stay focused on an activity. Children's attention span depends on many factors, the most

significant being their level of interest. Concentration depends on:

- ✓ the child's level of well-being (see Leuven Scale, page 10)
- ✓ the child's level of involvement (see Leuven Scale, page 11)
- ✓ whether the activity is chosen by the child or adult
- ✓ the proximity of others, adults and children
- ✓ the interaction and play with other children
- ✓ the interaction with the adult
- ✓ other distractions
- ✓ the time of day and the child's rhythm of rest and play

- **Ensure children are feeling ok**, by consciously considering Leuven's levels of well-being. Their concentration depends on how good they feel about themselves, how happy they feel and their feelings of belonging.

- **Use the principles of SOUL to approach children's play** (High/Scope 1998). We sometimes interact without being sufficiently aware of the child's own agenda and purpose. So, before you begin to interact, use SILENCE, OBSERVATION, UNDERSTANDING and LISTENING to ensure that you understand what the child is doing and trying to do. You can then assess how best to interact, whether for example to play alongside, to remain quiet, to comment or to provide help with resources etc. The adult can either increase involvement and attention levels through meaningful interaction, or reduce their engagement by intervening and breaking the child's concentration. **Appropriate interaction is the key!**

■ **Share books!** One to one and as a small group. An adult sharing a book can grab the attention of most children. Very young babies focus on black and white patterns and contrasts, and soon enjoy pictures of familiar things, books with sounds and things to touch. Young children love to hear familiar stories again and again, and listening and joining in stories develops all the skills in the **Communication Climbing Frame**.

There is a table on page 26 that shows the typical development of attention span from the baby to the 5 year old. This is a helpful reference to ensure you have realistic expectations when evaluating the extent of children's attention skills.

During a group session, many children can find it difficult to sit and listen for more than a few minutes. It is therefore important to make group times as active as possible by giving the children regular movement breaks that fit in with your activity. For example, act out parts of the story and pretend to be the rocket that takes off, '5..4..3..2..1.. Blast off!' Or do an action song that links to the story, such as 'Zoom to the moon'.

In group times:

■ **Keep activities short, simple and interesting** so all children can take part and complete them successfully.

■ **Be sensitive to the signs of children's boredom.** If the children start to fidget, nudge each other, yawn or turn around, these are signs that they need a change of activity and some movement!

■ **Position yourself close to the children who struggle to concentrate at group time**, they will have a clearer view of resources, have more immediate access to you and the activity, which may help them to be less distracted by the other children and things that they see.

■ **Enable children to be relaxed and comfortable** when they are listening and paying attention. If you place too much emphasis on 'good listening' or 'good sitting', some children concentrate so hard on 'sitting correctly' and looking in the right direction that they focus on this alone rather than the actual activity. In these cases, pleasing the adult becomes more important to them than the intended listening activity.

■ **Remain positive** (*Principle 6: Keep it positive*)
Consider how you can develop your skills of leading a group session; learn from each other. Always remain positive, relaxed and responsive to the needs of the children; go with the flow, rather than trying to 'control' them into behaving well. You want them to listen because they are interested and enjoying this time. Expected norms of behaviour will naturally develop because they want to join in and listen to you and each other.

Consider these 2 group time scenarios. Which group paid the most attention and developed their listening skills? Why?

Practitioner Nicole:

'Come and sit down now, let's see who is sitting nicely! Sureen sits with her legs crossed and arms folded, lifting them high so that Nicole can see her. 'Good sitting Sureen, let's see who can sit up straight like Sureen, well done Rama and Noah, excellent sitting!' There is a bit of shuffling as children find a space and Otis lies on his tummy with his chin in his hands. 'Come on Otis sit properly like everyone else', Otis slowly and reluctantly swivels onto his bottom. Evie is busy chatting to her friend. Nicole says, 'come on Evie, stop talking now and when everyone is quiet we'll listen to the story of the Hungry Caterpillar'. Nicole waits for everyone to stop talking, some children start fidgeting, Nicole eventually begins the story. Sureen is still sitting with her arms folded, as are a few others. Nicole breaks off the story at times to stop children talking, encouraging them to use their 'listening ears'.

Reflection

What do you mean by 'good sitting' and 'good listening'? Do you need to use these phrases at all? A child may be listening really well as she lies on her tummy and looks at the floor.

Practitioner Jody:

Gathers the group together, and as they are settling into the area for group activities, she says, 'who would like to hear the story about the Billy Goats Gruff and the Troll? Let's pretend we are the Billy Goats trip trapping over the bridge'. 'We need a bridge' says Aloni. Jody says, 'What shall we use for the bridge?' There is a bit of a discussion and they decide on the large wooden blocks and a plank. Jody sets up the bridge with some help from the children and splits the group into 2 halves, half Billy goats and half trolls. The children are excited and begin to mumble 'trip trap trip trap' and do the actions, some standing up, some using their hands on the ground. Jody gains their attention by saying 'great trip trapping! Let's begin the story and see if we can all do it together! Let's all start by sitting down with our hands on our knees, ready to join in the trip trapping. Altogether, 'trip trap, trip trap over the bridge!' All the children tap their hands on their legs in rhythm. 'And remember what the troll says?' says Jody, 'Yes!!' Shouted 2 or 3 children, 'all together then', says Jody, 'I'm a troll eeoll eeoll and I'm coming to eat you up!' Jody tells the story and the children are enthralled as they wait for their role to take part. The Billy goats trip trap in 3s over the bridge, and the trolls pop up their head with their horns and chant their lines.

3. Create the best environment

Early years settings are busy places. By nature there are many children, plenty of toys and resources and there is always a certain level of noise. This can make it difficult for children to give an activity their full attention or to listen to what you are saying to them.

You can make some small changes to your environment that will help the children to improve their attention and listening skills more easily:

- **Consider the number of toys and activities available** for children at any one time. Sometimes there can be too much choice and too many exciting activities available. Children can find it very difficult to settle on an activity if there are too many choices and they will flit from one area to another. Try to strike a balance between familiar toys, play areas and novelty.

- **Consider how you can reduce the general 'spread' of noise** in your learning areas. Think about creating smaller spaces within a large area, using drapes and portable screens, perhaps shrubs outdoors. Elizabeth Jarman (2009) says, *'in a space where every decision is made for you, where noise is all pervasive and an overload of resources are assaulting your senses, it's very hard to focus and think for yourself'*.
  Soft furnishings will reduce noise levels if the ceilings are high.

- **Create a space for a 'focus' activity**. For example, within a seating area of logs, or a den created with sheets, place a rucksack, binoculars, and a compass, maybe a book about exploring. This should capture the children's imagination and attention ready to begin a discovery activity. Other things can be used such as a dinosaur and some stones, a bus and some people. Or anything that connects with children's interests and your plans for developing their learning. (Idea from Jarman, 2009)

- **Consider your displays**. If walls are too busy they can be a distraction for some children and affect their concentration. Some children may suffer from visual overload. Review your displays, they are an important part of your overall environment. Ask yourselves how they enhance your environment, reflect children's learning, add to children's learning, and provide parental information. Consider the colours, format, interactive nature, and whether each one is unique, and purposeful.

- **Use outdoors!** There are so many things to listen to, to see and to hold children's attention! From experience, some children are more communicative outdoors, there is more to talk about! You may find, from your own experience, that when out walking with friends and family you communicate and chat more easily!

- **Use a wide range of open-ended resources** indoors and outdoors, such as sand, water and loose materials, for example, crates, ropes, tyres, planks etc. so that children can choose how to use them and create

their own challenges. This will keep them self-motivated. Introduce heuristic play by creating treasure baskets for babies, and a wide range of open-ended natural resources for toddlers (See Get active: Activities 11 and 12)

- **Ensure various levels of success** when planning more focused activities, so that all children feel they have accomplished something through their concentrated efforts.

- **Use a visual timetable** throughout the day. Visual timetables show children what will be happening throughout the session, in a way that they can understand. They are particularly useful for children who have difficulties with waiting, completing activities or who may wonder when their mum/main carer is coming back.

- **Reduce background noise as much as possible**. Avoid having background music such as nursery rhymes. This makes it difficult for everyone to listen and talk to each other. Wait until the children have gone home before you start the dishwasher or use the hoover because it is really hard to concentrate on something if there is too much noise. Get to know those children who don't like a lot of noise. They may get upset at times like lunchtime when the noise level naturally rises, so take them outside or to a quiet place to calm them, and communicate with them.

- **If noise levels rise**, try lowering your voices; talking quietly often prompts a quiet response from children, because they naturally mirror your manner and tone.

4. Work with parents

Let parents know about their child's progress with attention, concentration and listening, describing the activity and how they took part. For example, 'we did a listening walk, didn't we Jamal, and you heard the blackbird singing and the big lorry'.

Raise awareness about the importance of limiting 'screen time' and turning off the television when playing with their children and during meal times. Perhaps put a poster on your notice board, or mention this in your newsletter.

Share any concerns about hearing. If a child doesn't always respond to their name, or responds with 'what?' when you speak to them, ask parents whether or not the child's hearing has been checked within the past few months. Recommend that they ask their GP for a referral to the local audiology service, if the child's hearing has not recently been assessed.

Glue ear is particularly common in pre-school aged children. This is essentially fluid within the middle ear that impacts on the child's ability to hear. Glue ear can have a huge impact on a child's communication development if it is not picked up in the early stages. However, if it is identified, this can be monitored and attended to so that development is not hindered.

5. Support children who are learning EAL

The way in which you would support a child learning EAL with attention and listening is essentially the same way that you would support a monolingual child.

Keep your language simple for children with very limited English, and emphasise the key words in the sentence to convey the meaning.

Use a lot of non-verbal communication such as pointing and gestures to support what you are saying. This will make it easier for children learning EAL to understand, remain engaged and listen.

Respect the 'silent period' many children go through as they adjust to their new surroundings.
'All the time these children will be watching and listening and gradually taking in the English language that is being used around them' (Sargent, 2016, 11)

Use a lot of visual support to gain and maintain attention, such as, demonstrations, illustrations and real objects that show clearly what is happening and what the activity or story is about. For example, use a plate to show that it is lunchtime.

Make your environment welcoming and inclusive, by having resources and images that are familiar to the children, enabling them to feel comfortable. This will help them to become more engaged with activities and people around them.

> *'Working with children who are [learning] EAL is not just about language, it is also about identity and culture. In order to provide for these children you will need to create a welcoming and inclusive learning environment where all children are respected and valued and where all children feel comfortable, secure and proud of their linguistic heritage'.* (Sargent, 2016)

Case study: Yui, 4 years, 6 months
Yui is in reception. She is of Japanese ethnicity.

Yui settled very well into reception at the start of the academic year.

For a while, Yui's teacher, Miss Kennedy had noticed that Yui very rarely looks at her. For example, when answering her name in the register and during carpet time, Yui does not make eye contact.

One day in particular, Miss Kennedy was concerned that Yui was not listening during group time, as she didn't seem to look at Miss Kennedy once. Miss Kennedy suspected that perhaps Yui was feeling bored.

The following day when Yui's mum came to pick Yui up from school, she had a brief chat with Miss Kennedy. Yui's mum said that Yui is really enjoying coming to school and especially learning about mini-beasts during group time.

Miss Kennedy then had a discussion with the Inclusion Manager at her school who made the point that different cultures have very different eye contact customs. In the Japanese culture, it can be a sign of disrespect if pupils look directly at a superior.

So Miss Kennedy learnt the valuable lesson that different cultures have different eye contact etiquette. Yui has simply been following the social norms of her Japanese culture by avoiding direct contact with her teacher. Although she does not look at the teacher, Miss Kennedy has been reassured that Yui definitely listens intently and enjoys the input in class.

Miss Kennedy plans to discuss this further with Yui's mum, to decide on the best way to help Yui settle in to the British way of life, and still maintain a strong identity with her Japanese heritage. She feels that Yui should understand that in the British culture, eye contact with adults is ok, and that it will help her to take a more active part in classroom activities.

6. Provide extra support for children with difficulties

It is likely that there will be some children in your setting who have difficulties with attention and listening. They might appear to be always 'on the go' and struggle to focus on an activity for more than a couple of minutes. They might also find it very hard to concentrate at group times.

Find out what interests and motivates them, just as you would with all children. Most children will be excited by something, whether it's cars, princesses, pirates or a more unusual interest. If you're not sure what a child loves, simply ask their parents. Once you know what really grabs the child's attention, you can incorporate this into a wide range of activities. For example, if you know the child loves cars, you can put out simple transport puzzles, set up a car wash or create a bus or a train out of large boxes.

Use 'Get Active' activities everyday with children to constantly improve their attention skills and motivate them to listen.

Case study: Laszlo, 3 years 2 months   PART 2
Laszlo is always 'on the go' and finds group times and snack time difficult when he is expected to sit still. He will often get up and go and play and his key person, Sam, encourages him to come back to the group. Laszlo flits from one activity to another very quickly and is easily distracted by anything that he can see and hear around him.

Sam spoke to Laszlo's mum to find out what he liked doing at home. He found out that he loved playing superheroes with his older brother. Staff agreed to try hard to make activities more appealing for Laszlo by using his love of superheroes as a theme when possible.

Laszlo helped to paint a big box black to make a 'Bat car' and Laszlo played in this for a long time alone and with other children. Staff make group times an active experience with lots of singing and actions, including superhero moves. They have noticed that Laszlo joins in enthusiastically when they are singing and acting things out. This has also been a big success for other children too!

Laszlo's attention span is improving.

Get active!

Activity 1: Ready, steady, go!

Why? This is an exciting way to help children to '**look, listen and wait**' for an instruction. They look at you and listen for you to say 'Ready, steady go!' before they do something exciting like roll a car down a ramp or run to a tree and back.

Ready, steady, go games are an easy introduction to adult-led activities and may help some children join in games with adults for the first time.

Resources: All sorts of toys for 'Ready, steady go!' games. Choose things that will excite the children. The possibilities are endless!

Examples of activities

Roll cars, balls, slinkies down ramps
Pour water from a large watering can into a bucket, use glitter or rice for pouring, splat your hand in shaving foam on a table
Race to a cone/fence/tree
Run and collect the bean bag from the hoop, or run and put it in the hoop

For younger children, start with cause and effect toys, such as pop up toys

How? You can do this with one child or a small group. You can set it up, or play the game with a child at their chosen activity, for example race cars with them

- Choose your motivating toy or activity and demonstrate what you want them to do
- Say 'Ready, steady go!' in an enthusiastic manner and then carry out the action yourself on the word 'go'. For example, drop a ball or car down the ramp or guttering when you say 'go'. Tell the child 'your turn' and tell them, 'wait for 'go'. Then simply follow with 'Ready, steady, go!'

Some children will have no problem waiting for 'go'. Others will start the activity as soon as they have it in their hand. If they struggle to wait for you to say 'go', try putting your hand gently over their hand until you say 'go'!

Acknowledge what the child has done with enthusiasm, and say, 'you waited for the go!'

Helpful hint: Once the children have mastered 'Ready, steady, go' games, you can pause between each word for longer, for example, 'Ready...(pause)...steady...(pause)... go! This means that the children have to wait, look, listen and maintain their focus of attention for longer.

Helpful hint: For extra fun, use other words instead of 'go' sometimes. For example, say 'Ready steady bananas!' or 'Ready steady sausages!' The children still have to wait until they hear the word 'go' before they act!

Activity 2: Musical statues

Why? Musical statues requires the children to **listen** carefully for the music to stop when they are dancing. This game gives the children practice at listening when they are moving, hence doing two things at the same time.

Resources: Plenty of space for the children to dance, music!

How? Explain to the children that they have to stand still when the music stops
- Start off with a couple of practice rounds to check that all of the children understand the game
- Start the music and encourage the children to dance
- Stop the music and become a statue yourself to demonstrate, go large with funny faces and poses! Check that everyone is trying to be as still as possible as they strike their pose
- Then restart the music.

Helpful hint: You can also play musical bumps (where the children have to sit down on the floor as quickly as possible when the music stops). This is an easier game for younger children and is easy to develop into musical statues.

Activity 3: Find the noisy toy

Why? Listening for the location of a sound encourages children to sustain their attention on a sound. It also supports them to focus on one sound in particular while blocking out other noises. This game also promotes completing an activity, particularly if the child likes the toy.

Resources: Gather a selection of musical toys that make an ongoing noise.

How?
- Choose a toy that makes an ongoing noise and show it to a group of children
- Tell the children to turn around or close their eyes, another adult may be helpful here!
- Hide the musical toy somewhere in the room
- When you say go, the children listen carefully to try and find the toy
- Start in a small room or a small area of a room
- Move to a bigger space if and when you feel the children are ready.

For younger children, set up a few blankets and hide a toy under one of the blankets. You will need to put other items under the spare blankets so that the children won't be able to tell which blanket the toy is under just by looking.

Helpful hint: The children can also take turns to hide the item.

Get active!

Activity 4: Go on a listening walk

Why? A listening walk is a great opportunity for children to practise **listening** in a fun way. It is a practical way of showing the children how to listen well. By the end of the listening walk, the children will have heard and listened to a range of sounds, some loud and some quiet, some familiar and some unfamiliar. As well as learning about the wonders of nature and the everyday world, it will help them to understand that they need to be still and quiet in order to listen really carefully.

Resources: A planned walking route on the site of your early years setting. This might be a simple loop around the outside area, down the corridor and back to your room. It is great if you can take the children outside for part of the listening walk.

Optional: Gather a selection of photographs to represent sounds that you are likely to hear, for example, a car, someone talking, children laughing, birds tweeting, a bell ringing, a door shutting, children playing, a dog barking, shoes, footsteps, a bird, a bee, a printer, the buzzing sound of the fridge, a phone ringing.

How?

- Listening walks work best with small groups of children (maximum of 8 children)
- Explain that you will be going on a 'listening walk' to find out what you can hear
- Ask the children what is the best way to listen? (Stop, stand still, be quiet and listen)
- Walk around the planned route, stopping every few metres to listen
- Talk about the sounds that they hear
- Use the photographs to help children to understand what the sounds are, as you won't always see the source of the sound
- Encourage the children to imitate the sounds they hear
- Encourage children to describe the sound, loud, quiet, short, long, sharp
- After your listening walk, talk about the sounds that you heard and what helped the children to listen.

Helpful hint: Let parents know about the walk and what they heard so they can chat about it with their children.

Activity 5: Copy me

Why? Children have to **listen** carefully to copy a sound, the beats and rhythm the adult makes with tap sticks or a musical instrument.

Resources: Tap sticks, a tambourine or a drum. It will help if children have their own instrument

How? 'Copy me' sound games work best when you have two adults to demonstrate it to the children first
- Say to the other adult 'first listen, then copy'. Then tap a certain number of beats (1, 2 or 3 beats) The adult copies the sound. Do this again with a different beat to show children another example
- Let the children take it in turns to copy the number of beats and rhythm that you play
- If the children are able to do this, try a harder rhythm.

Helpful hint: Have a go at this activity using clapping rather than a musical instrument. Let the children lead the beat or rhythm for everyone to copy.

Activity 6: What's wrong with the song?

Why? Encouraging children to spot errors in songs and rhymes encourages them to **listen** more attentively to every word that you are saying.

Resources: Your voice!
It's also great if you use puppets for this activity.

How?
- Choose a nursery rhyme that the children know very well
- Sing the song as a group with the children
- Then tell them to listen as the puppet sings the song
- The children listen while you sing the nursery rhyme in the character as the puppet
- Add in one or two errors and ask the children to tell you when they spot something wrong.

Helpful hint: Make the errors obvious at the start, for example, 'Baa baa black chicken...'. Once the children have spotted a few obvious errors, make them less obvious, for example, use words that rhyme, such as 'three blind dice'.

Activity 7: Assault Course

Why? This helps children **to pay attention** to 2 things at once. They have to listen for a noise while they concentrate on doing something physical.

Resources: A large space! A cleared room, a hall or outside area.
Equipment for an assault course for example, mats, benches, hoops, bean bags, bucket, barrel, tunnel, soft play.
Something that makes a loud noise, for example, a bell or drum.

How?
- Set up an assault course, either in a line or a circuit that children clamber over, under, along and through
- Demonstrate how to use each piece of equipment
- Explain they travel along the course and when they hear a special sound they have to do a special action. Children can take turns one at a time, if the course is short, or they can begin a little way after each other with all children moving at the same time. Always keep waiting to a minimum
- Introduce the listening activity by playing the sound they need to listen out for, the bell or drum
- Tell them to do an action when they hear the sound. For example, touch their toes, clap their hands, or stop
- Demonstrate the activity on the assault course and responding to the sound of the bell or drum.

Helpful hint: Have a manageable number of children on the circuit, so there is no waiting.
Encourage children to be quiet as they move so that they can hear the sound.

Get active!

Activity 8: Ribbon dance

Why? Children will develop their **attention skills** as they copy the adult's movements with the ribbon stick.

Resources: Space and ribbon sticks.

How? Make sure the children have plenty of space around them and do not touch each other when they stretch their arms out to the sides

- Demonstrate an up and down movement with your ribbon and say 'up and down and up and down and...' as you move the ribbon up and down
- Encourage all of the children to copy you
- Then change from up and down movements to side to side movements (left to right) and say 'side to side and side to side...'.
- Once all the children are copying you, switch between the up and down movements and the side to side movements without words, and see if the children can stay focused and copy
- Use different ribbon movements, such as waving it above your head, swirling it around your legs and making big circles in front of your body.

Helpful hint: Make big arm movements to make the ribbon float and make shapes.

Activity 9: Exercises to music

Why? This is a really enjoyable way for children to **look, focus and concentrate** as they try to copy your movements.

Resources: A lively piece of music you like with a good beat.

How? Develop a range of simple exercises using all the body parts. Consider all the limbs and joints and what they can do:

- Legs - bend, stretch, lift and kick in all directions, walk, skip, run in all directions
- Arms - lift, reach, circle in all directions, wave, stretch out to the sides, move out and in
- Hands – clap, wave, circle, twinkle by opening and closing the hand, punch, click
- Feet – kick, tap, stamp, jump, stretch, open out to the side and close into the body
- Hips – wiggle, circle, bend up and down
- Shoulders – lift and lower (together, separate), circle
- Knees and elbows – bend and stretch
- Choose simple moves and repeat the sequence, counting to 4 or 8
- Choose 3 sequences and repeat these so the children get to know them.

Helpful hint: Begin with easy moves like wiggling hips from side to side, bending knees, then add on a clap or arm movement, once they have mastered the first move.

Activity 10: Round and round, roly-polys!

Why? Vestibular activities prompt brain activity and development.

Resources: Depending on the activity below – lively music, or soft gentle music, a pile of cushions and a yoga mat.

How? Dance, dance, dance! Twirl and swing to music and have fun with children!
- Dance with children in your arms, and together holding hands with their feet on the ground
- Twizz them around holding underneath their arms
- Roll down hills
- Wrap them in a yoga mat and let them unravel as they roll down a pile of cushions!
- 2 children lie down on their backs head to head, with bodies lying away from each other. Reach over their heads and hold hands. Then roll sideways together along mats or a carpet or on the grass.

Helpful hint: Use hard floors for spinning around on your bottom. Go one way and then the other way when spinning to counteract the dizziness! Ask children how they feel, what is happening when they stop.

Activity 11: Heuristic play - treasure baskets (from 6-8 months, when babies can sit unaided)

Why? Heuristic play for babies stimulates the senses, because it is about providing them with different textures and materials to explore that are not plastic. The different feel of the materials stimulates their brain into working out what things do, how they feel, and what is different. This deepens their concentration and extends their attention span.

Resources: A basket made from natural material, preferably round and low sided. Objects are from the 'real world' and from a variety of sources in nature and the around the house. Here is an example of objects, more ideas can be found at:
http://www.mheducation.co.uk/openup/chapters/9780335246441.pdf
http://baby-brain.co.uk/treasure-baskets-and-heuristic-play/
http://www.thecreationstationstore.co.uk/downloads/baby-treasure-basket.pdf
'The Little Book of Treasure Baskets' by Anne Roberts and Sally Featherstone

The original idea of treasure baskets has been developed by various people into providing themed baskets, of colours, shapes, and materials, such as round things, green things, black and white things, wooden things etc. All these ideas are excellent for captivating children's attention by stimulating deep thought processes.

A quick list:
Tin with something in like a pebble to rattle
Various brushes – nail, bath, hair, toothbrush
Ball – large enough not to go in the mouth!

Pine cone	Large shell
Ribbons	Scarf
Thick beaded necklace	Wooden toy
Peg	Wooden box with lid

Large stone	Furry fabric
Wooden spoon	Wooden brick
Curtain hoop	Jar top
Metal chain	Small mirror
Feather	Shower scrubber
Cork	

How? This is a discovery activity for babies, so the most important thing is that the baby chooses what to play with and how to play with it.
It is also essential that the adult is in close proximity to the child, for reassurance and safety reasons. As the items are everyday household and natural things, there is no 'safety guarantee' as with bought toys.
Use the basket at certain times of the day, when there are no other distractions.
Sit quietly with the baby and watch as they choose and discover what things feel like, taste like, sound like, how heavy they feel, sharp or soft, scratchy or bumpy.
Don't intervene, unless invited or for safety reasons, and remain quiet so that they are not distracted by your interaction.

Health and safety: Check items for safety, regularly wash and wipe items as they will have been in babies' mouths

Helpful hint: Regularly add to and change the items in the basket, or have a range of baskets with different items to rotate. Babies can play with these resources for around 30 minutes or more!

Activity 12: Heuristic play for toddlers

Why? This is discovery play for toddlers, using their ever-developing skills of 'posting', 'putting inside', 'on' or 'under', piling things up, knocking them down, moving things about, rolling things around, and covering things. It prolongs concentration, through thinking and discovering.

Resources: Draw string bags to put resources inside, baskets and tins for resources, natural resources that children can use for the skills mentioned above, resources such as:
Wooden toilet roll holder or pole with curtain rings and bangles for stacking
An assortment of boxes and tubes
Boxes that fit inside each other
Tubes that fit inside each other and stones or natural items to post through them
Collections of fir cones, shells, corks, tubes, and natural or metal containers for enabling the sorting, moving things from place to place and handling
A variety of metal spoons, whisks, sieves
Curtain rings with different coloured ribbons attached
Metal chains of different thickness...and much more!

More ideas can be found at: https://uk.pinterest.com/explore/heuristic-play/?lp=true

How?
Have space and a special time for this discovery play, and clear away other toys to eliminate distractions.
Resources can be shared.
Allow children to play as they wish with the resources, and observe what they do, you will discover their schemas, (patterns of thinking), and see them work things out.

Helpful hint: Always have an adult close by to check on safety issues with these resources.
Clear away the resources together, perhaps as a sorting activity.

Tables of development

Typical development of attention skills

0-1 year - Fleeting attention

Children are highly distractible and their attention is fleeting. This means that their attention flits from one thing to another, depending on what is happening around them, for example, turning when someone walks in the room, or to the sound of a door banging.

Within a child's first year, they develop joint attention (shared attention). Joint attention occurs when a child is sharing the focus on something with another person. For example, if an adult points at a dog, the child would look at the dog then back at the adult.

1-2 years - Rigid attention

Children concentrate on a task or activity of their own choice for short periods. When concentrating on an activity, they will not usually respond if you call their name or attempt to talk to them, however they will usually look if you touch them to speak to them. The child may seem to be ignoring you, but they have not yet developed the ability to attend to more than one stimulus at a time, for example, doing a puzzle while listening. All of their attention is focused on their task.

Children of this age often struggle to follow directions from adults and they may be upset when an adult intervenes with their focused play.

2-3 years - Single-channeled attention

Children can still only focus on one task at a time, however their attention becomes more flexible. With help from an adult, children can shift their attention. For example, they will look up from their puzzle and listen to you without too much difficulty, if touched. They will then look back at their puzzle if you point towards the puzzle. Children aged 2-3 years are also more able to focus on activities that are not of their choosing.

3-4 years - Focusing attention

Between the ages of 3-4 years, children can switch the focus of their attention without help from an adult. So if they are stacking blocks, for example, and you give a verbal instruction, they can stop stacking blocks while they listen to you and then return to stacking blocks independently. They are not yet able to listen while stacking blocks, they must stop the activity in order to listen.

4-5 years - Two-channeled attention

By the time children reach 5 years of age, they are likely to have developed two-channeled attention. This means that they can pay attention to more than one thing at the same time. By this age, they do not always need to stop an activity to listen. For example, if you speak to a child of this age while he is stacking bricks, he should be able to listen to you whilst continuing to stack the blocks.

(Based on Cooper, Moodley and Reynell, 1978)

Tables of development

Attention span by age. (Helen Fowler Neville, 2007)

Age	Activity	How Can We Help?
2 to 7 months	A baby may watch someone, copy expressions and sounds for as long as 2-3 minutes at 2 months. By 7 months, this typically continues for at least 5 minutes.	Take turns leading and following. Be warm, interested, and interesting to look at. Notice when babies have had enough and turn away.
18 months	Alone, a toddler may spend 30 seconds on a single activity or a minute or two on several activities before seeking the caregiver's attention.	Be available, understanding and ready with other activities.
2 years	Alone, a 2 year old may spend 30-60 seconds on a single activity; with an adult's active encouragement, 2-3 minutes or longer.	By playing with toddlers or talking about their activities, adults can increase children's attention spans.
2½ years	Alone, the toddler may spend about 2 minutes on a single activity. The usual preference is for almost constant attention from an adult. With or near a small group of children, a toddler may play peacefully for 10 minutes.	Point out characteristics of whatever they are playing with by commenting: 'Look, there is a pattern on the paper', 'I can see a black dot in the centre', 'it seems to have a tiny hole at the back'.
3 years	A child playing alone may spend 3-8 minutes on an interesting activity and may finish it if it's easy.	Look for ways to keep young children interested in the activities they start. Encourage and follow their interests. Be sensitive to joining their play; Use S.O.U.L. to enter children's play (See Section 2).
3½ years	Playing alone, a child can stay busy for 15 minutes if there are a variety of interesting choices, some children may spend longer engrossed in make believe with small figures.	
4 years	By 4, a child engrossed in an activity may ignore distractions such as the call to dinner. Alone, the 4 year old may spend 7-8 minutes on a single activity, or as much as 15 minutes if the activity is new, especially interesting, and if they have to work things out; this engages their critical thinking. With a small group, a 4 year old may spend 5-10 minutes playing without interruption.	Make the tasks achievable and interesting in adult-led activities. Use resources they like, and tune into their passions. Keep children interested in projects with impromptu games and humour.
4½ years	On their own, the child may spend 2-3 minutes on a task chosen by an adult such as getting dressed or picking up toys.	
5 years	By 5, most children can ignore minor distractions. Alone, they will focus on a single interesting activity for 10 or 15 minutes and on an assigned task for 4-6 minutes if it's easy and interesting. A small group of children can work or play together without interruption for 10-25 minutes.	Tune in to children's interests and passions! Recognise that personal interest remains the most important motivation for 5 year olds. It will double the length of their attention span.

Section 2: Active Social Communication

Why is it important?

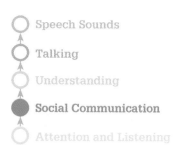

- Speech Sounds
- Talking
- Understanding
- **Social Communication**
- Attention and Listening

'Communication is the 'must have' skill for children and young people and is the bedrock of learning.' (Royal College of Speech and Language Therapists, 2012)

'Social and communication skills are reciprocal; improving one triggers the development of the other.' (Goldstein et al. 2002)

This section is about how children develop the skills to communicate socially with others. It is about communicating in a reciprocal way, expecting the other person to understand and respond to what you say and do, and for you to understand and respond to what they say and do. There is a social engagement and a shared attention to someone or something in order for it to happen. To understand what someone is saying, which is the next stage on the **Communication Climbing Frame**, ideally, children need to connect with that person and so require the necessary social skills. Most of these skills are non-verbal.

Take a look at the **Communication Chain** (page 5). Social communication skills feature in several places because they are required for understanding someone's speech as well as to communicating a message yourself. The whole process of communication is a social activity and requires social skills. A large part of the social communication skills in the chain is interpreting non-verbal communication from the speaker and using appropriate gestures and facial expressions when getting a message across yourself. We need to remember that children are generally very sensitive to our body language and facial expressions and learn to interpret these body language and facial expressions much earlier than they do language.

It is worth remembering that many aspects of our social communication are unique to our British culture. Children learn skills from birth as they interact with their main carers. Children growing up in different cultures may have developed different ways of communicating socially.

> *'There is a wide range of acceptable norms within and across individuals, families, and cultures. For example, preferences for maintaining or averting eye contact, expectations for adult-child interactions, or norms for personal space may vary.'* (www.asha.org, 2017)

Our aim in early years is to respect and understand different cultural norms and to help children to become competent and confident within the British culture.

Playing is what children do and is the main way children learn to be sociable and to communicate. Since *'play and communication skills develop hand in hand'* (Pepper and Weitzman, 2004), it is important to understand the developmental milestones for both play and social communication. It is helpful to refer to these to check the stage and progress of your key children, and to know what to expect from them next. Knowing these stages will help direct your level and type of interaction and guide your planning.

The expectations for children at the end of the EYFS for social communication skills are in the EYFS section on Personal, social and emotional development (PSED), as being able to communicate with others is part of their social development.

These early learning goals give us a clear picture of our young children's capabilities. They are gaining vital life skills that stay with them forever, and determine how they will manage healthy relationships in the future.

Reflection

Think about what makes a successful conversation between two adults. Remember that conversations are not just about the words we use and listening, there are many other factors that make a conversation work well.

Statutory Framework for the EYFS (2017) Early Learning Goals PSED

Managing feelings and behaviour: children talk about how they and others show feelings, talk about their own and others' behaviour, and its consequences, and know that some behaviour is unacceptable. They work as part of a group or class, and understand and follow the rules. They adjust their behaviour to different situations, and take changes of routine in their stride.

Making relationships: children play co-operatively, taking turns with others. They take account of one another's ideas about how to organise their activity. They show sensitivity to others' needs and feelings, and form positive relationships with adults and other children.

What is social communication?

Social communication is a term that refers to how we communicate. It is about how we use language and non-verbal communication to communicate with others. It is all about communicating in socially appropriate ways.

Let's look at the dynamics of a simple conversation.

Here are some things you may have thought about:
- stand or sit an 'appropriate distance' away from the person you are communicating with
- use 'appropriate eye contact' which Bowen describes as 'not too much staring, and not too much looking away during a conversation'

- take turns with the other speaker in conversation
- tune-in to the feelings of others by interpreting facial expressions, body language, tone of voice, etc.
- know what is and what is not an appropriate comment to make
- introduce topics of conversation
- be able to *'distinguish how to talk and behave towards different communicative partners.'* (Bowen, 1998)

Many of these are examples of non-verbal social communication skills, which are some of the skills we are helping children to develop. Communication is about much more than just using words.

> *'At least 50% of the message conveyed is through non-verbal communication.'* (Elks and McLachlan, 2015)

> *'Successful communicators know the unspoken rules of conversation, which include waiting and listening while someone else speaks and then following up with a comment or a question that relates back to what the speaker has just said. We all need to learn these unspoken rules of conversation to become effective communicators.'* (Sussman, 2016)

It takes time to learn the rules of interactions!

In the early years it is only expected that children are able to follow some 'social rules'. By the time a child is 5 years of age, they usually have a good grasp of social rules such as making eye contact and using facial expressions to match what they are saying. They can also share items and take-turns some of the time. Other social communication skills are not usually mastered until a little bit later in childhood. For example, 5 year olds don't always know what they should and shouldn't say in a situation, often being the cause of embarrassment to parents in public places!

These are the social communication skills that we can expect children to develop in the early years:

- Smiling back when smiled at
- Responding consistently upon hearing their name
- Showing an interest in other children
- Interacting with peers
- Playing with others
- Making appropriate eye contact
- Taking turns with toys and other items
- Sharing
- Being able to get the attention of an adult
- Greeting familiar people
- Pretend play
- Initiating interactions
- Appropriate proximity (i.e. not getting too close when talking to someone)

- Asking for help in an appropriate way
- Being able to wait (e.g. waiting for their turn)
- Being able to make choices
- Joining in
- Coping with winning and losing

The better a child is at being social, the better their chances of working their way to the top of the **Communication Climbing Frame** to become confident and successful communicators, and this starts from birth. Several studies have shown that the more socially engaged a baby is, the better their chances are of developing good communication skills. Moreover, Hamer (National Literacy Trust, 2012) states that the more a baby uses gesture to initiate interactions, the earlier they are likely to start using words.

Children who have difficulties socially or who are delayed in this area often have difficulties talking. This is because if they find it hard to approach others to play, they have fewer opportunities to practise communicating and talking. These children face many challenges as they work their way to the top of the **Communication Climbing Frame**, but early years practitioners can have a huge positive impact on this development by interacting sensitively, organising the environment and activities well and most importantly, helping children to develop friendships.

Non-Verbal Communication

Non-verbal communication is about what we do with our face and body, for example, using eye contact, nodding, smiling, frowning, clenching hands together, moving our

hands around, shrugging shoulders and standing at an appropriate distance. Children also show their delight and excitement by jumping and dancing around!

Surprisingly, the way we use our voice (apart from using words) is also classed as 'non-verbal communication', which includes the tone of voice, how loud or quiet we are, laughing, grunting, whether we talk fast or slow, and, for example, when we 'sound' as if we are annoyed, even though the words may not say that we are!

Children absorb so much from just being with the adults who care for them on how to behave towards others and communicate appropriately. However, this also means they will absorb inappropriate non-verbal communication too!

Most babies are social little beings with very expressive faces, who communicate with us successfully through their non-verbal communication. You can tell if they are content or if they are experiencing discomfort by their facial expressions as well as the noises they make. Babies are drawn to look at the faces of their caregivers:

> 'Being interested in his mother is the first step a baby takes toward becoming a social being.' (Sussman, 2016)

In order for a baby to become a social little being, adult interaction is key. Babies need to have endless opportunities to experience this 'dance of social communication'. They learn to recognise facial expressions, such as those of animated joy and excitement when they do something new like rolling over, and then the more serious and calm face when they are feeding, for example. In this way they begin to 'read' people's responses, copy expressions and attune their own needs to the person who is with them. The huge importance of social communication is emphasised by Gopnick and colleagues who suggest that the brain can be thought of as a 'social brain', one which is developed through social interaction, particularly the relationship between parent and child. (Hamer/National Literacy Trust, 2012)

See page 42 for typical developmental milestones for social communication for babies from birth to 12 months old. (Based on Sheridan, 2008)

Communication styles

Social communication is about how we communicate. Pepper and Weitzman (2004) identified four Communication Styles in children that depend on their personality, how comfortable they feel in a situation, physical health, competence in language and overall development.

> 'A child's communication style can make it easier or harder for her to interact with others.' (Pepper and Weitzman, 2004)

The Four Communication Styles

Sociable Communication Style	• Will often start interactions • Responds easily when others interact with them • Even if they are not able to use words yet, they try to interact with others • Finds it easy to take the lead in interaction
Reluctant Communication Style	• Does not often start interactions • It isn't always obvious that the child has communicated with you • Finds it easier to respond when others start the interaction • May need time to get used to someone before responding to that person
Passive Communication Style	• Rarely starts interactions or responds • Appears to show limited interest in people • May be unwell or take medication that make them tired. This affects their communication style
Own-agenda Communication Style	• Tends to play alone • Rarely starts interactions with others • Will start interactions when he needs something • does not respond easily to adult prompting

Children may move in and out of these different communication styles, depending on who they are with, how comfortable they feel and what they are doing. We all know chatty children who become non-communicative when in unfamiliar surroundings. If children constantly show some of the indicators for passive, reluctant or own agenda communication styles then they are likely to benefit from extra help and support. Children with a sociable communication style will fly with their learning when adults organise a communication rich environment and make talking fun.

Turn-taking

Turn-taking is fundamental to positive interactions. It is likely that we have all been on the receiving end of an adult who has not developed this skill too well, or who chooses not to use it! They tend to go on about themselves and their lives in a monologue, without showing an interest in you or your life. This is a key communication skill for us all!

Turn-taking starts early in the first few months of life when the baby makes a gesture or noise and receives or waits for a response from the care-giver. The baby naturally seeks interaction through babbling, facial expressions, and gestures, and adults respond with the same kind of vocalising and gesturing back. Adults repeat and extend the baby's communication through commenting on their actions and babbling. This back and forth process, shapes the developing brain of a baby and is known as contingency. Research links contingency with developing secure attachments, and also the linguistic skills of gestures, vocalisations, speech and syntax. (Hamer/National Literacy Trust, 2012). Turn-taking is therefore a vital social communication skill.

Turn-taking generally, with toys and activities, can strengthen children's understanding and ability to take turns listening and speaking. (Scarlett, Naudeau, Salonuis-Pasternak & Ponte, 2005.) When babies become toddlers, taking turns with peers with toys is a challenge! This is because *'until the age of three, children increasingly have preference for their own goals that can conflict with those of others requiring compromise and negotiation.'* (Hamer/National Literacy Trust, 2012). We all know that toddlers need a high level of support with sharing and turn-taking in early years settings, and even when they are older and understand 'sharing and taking turns', it is still so very hard to do! Children may understand turn-taking but often their impulses to want a particular toy overrides their better judgement! If we put this into context with our own sometimes uncontrollable impulses to buy that new dress (when we don't need it), or eat that cake (when we're on a diet) then we can easily identify with their impulsive behaviour!

As adults you must remember that we don't enjoy queuing and waiting our turn, it is often frustrating and boring. It is best, therefore, to reduce the times that children experience this throughout the day, during everyday routines for toileting and eating, for example. Help children to understand and manage this difficult skill of taking turns through playing fun games and natural social play situations, rather than tedious waiting. During sand play, for example, there should be enough spades, rakes and other tools for everyone, but children may need help allowing each other to use the different tools, by exchanging them.

By the end of the EYFS, it is expected that most children have shown good progress with turn-taking and can take turns often, but they will still need help in many situations.

Friendships

Making friends is crucial to the development of social communication skills. The skills we develop for making friends are used throughout our lives. Hartup (1992) believes that how children adapt to life as adults, is not so dependent on their academic success or how they behave in settings and schools, but how they get on with other children.

The ability to make friends starts from birth, as already mentioned, with the attachment relationship between the baby and parents. Children who have had warm and trusting relationships are more likely to have a positive sense of themselves and are more likely to make friendships with other children. (Geddes, 2006)

Making friends is all about developing relationships. The DfE Guidance document, 'Early Years Outcomes (2013), refers to the developmental stages children go through in making relationships. From young babies responding when talked to (birth-11 months), to older babies building relationships with special people (8-20 months), to toddlers playing alongside each other (16-26 months) and starting to join in play with others (22-36 months), to pre-schoolers and children in reception classes playing in a group (30-50 months) and playing cooperatively with other children (40-60+ months).

Friendship skills and social skills are developed as children play and there are clear stages of play that children go through from birth. Being aware of these stages helps to guide practice in terms of expectations, resources and interactions.

Stages of play (Based on Parten, 1933)

Solitary	Child plays alone. There is limited interaction with other children
Spectator	Child observes other children playing nearby but does not join in play with them
Parallel	Child plays alongside other children, does not yet play with them
Associative	Child starts to interact with others in their play and there may be fleeting co-operation between children in play. Develops friendships and the preferences for playing with certain children. Play is normally in mixed sex groups
Co-operative	Child plays together with peers in a shared play context. Play can be more complicated and children will support each other in developing the play scenario. Child tends to play in single sex groups from 4½-5 years.

The ages that children move through these stages differs according to the child and their social experiences, but generally, children under 2 years take part in solitary, spectator and parallel play, and between 2½ and 4 years develop associate play. Cooperative play usually develops between 3½ and 6 years, becoming more complex with age.

The interaction between the adult and child at each stage of play has a major influence on developing friendship skills. For example, during parallel play, an adult can draw attention to what each child is doing to help them be aware of each other and their play. Adults can help children include others in their complex fantasy play through sensitive intervention, and help children to manage their inevitable disagreements.

Case Study: Abdul, 3 years old
Abdul seeks out the company of others and initiates interactions with familiar people. He also likes to play alone, making up stories with his small world figures.

He makes appropriate eye contact with other children and adults; he seeks cuddles when upset; he plays alongside other children or with other children, depending on the activity; he enjoys playing with a range of toys and particularly enjoys role play. He usually shares toys and takes turns without support from an adult. He recognises when other children are upset and attempts to comfort them.

Social communication skills are age-appropriate

Case study: Mikale, 3 years 2 months   PART 1
Mikale prefers to play alone. He rarely makes eye contact and regularly snatches toys from other children. He mainly plays with toy cars and has limited interest in other toys. He does not notice or respond when other children are upset. Mikale sometimes growls at other children.

Social communication skills are not age-appropriate

There is more information about the steps that staff have taken to support Mikale with his social communication
See Case study: Mikale PART 2, page 37

The adult role

'Parents, caregivers and early years professionals play a crucial role in supporting a child's social development. The emphasis should be on creating opportunities rather than direct teaching of skills.' (Sheridan, 2008)

1. Take an Active Approach

Do lots of physical activities!

Physical activities by their very nature are often social activities. Children play ball together or with an adult, they play hide and seek in a group, they negotiate space on large equipment, play games like chase and follow the leader. Group games help children to feel a sense of belonging and acceptance and there is often a feel-good factor about being in a group with a shared purpose.

You see children laughing and smiling joyfully as they play with a parachute, and dance and sing together. Doing these activities as adults usually has the same effect!

Dancing is a great way to be social; it stimulates us physically and emotionally, and releases more endorphins than any other activity according to Peter Lovatt, dance psychologist. Studies have shown that for adults, dancing increases happiness and creative thinking patterns. (Lovatt in Haliwell, 2016)

Physical activities are fun! Having fun is a wonderful social experience that is highly effective in helping children to learn and to remember that learning. *'When you're having fun together, you're helping him develop his communication skills.'* (Pepper and Weitzman, 2004)

2. Play and Interact

As a key person in the setting, you are vital to helping a child develop their social skills. As the person who understands the child best, you are able to nurture their social interactions sensitively, with a keen awareness of their character, their interests, their language skills and their daily feelings of well-being.

Be aware of:
- your own character traits and their impact
- when to be peaceful and when to be lively to suit the child's rhythm
- how best to share each other's character traits amongst your children so that they benefit from everyone's strengths
- when children naturally gravitate towards staff because they feel a connection.

Children copy intonation, accent and pronunciation, words, expressions, body language, emotions, movements, facial expressions. (Mirror neurons page 6)

As a result, social communication must be:
Clear – with open body language children can interpret easily, so they can see you are pleased to see them, and interested in what they are doing and saying

Respectful – with the same respect you would give to another adult

Polite – using good manners and with courtesy

Meaningful to that child – connecting to the child's experiences and level of understanding

Consistent – so that everyone has the same respectful approach to children

With eye contact – by getting down to the child's level and being completely engaged with them

Two-way - so that listening is as important to role model as speaking is; show a genuine interest in what the child is saying and doing and be captivated by them.

- **Be an excellent role model for children:** How you are with children has a huge impact on their social development, well-being and overall learning. It is all about making a connection! Be yourself, but be conscious of the good practice 'ways of being' below that are common to everyone to ensure consistency of approach and impact on the child.

Essential good practice – ways of being for everyone
There are ways of being that are consistent for all practitioners that will ensure children learn successfully and develop good communication and language skills.

Celebrate our differences!
We are all different in the way we interact because we all have different personalities, ways of talking and being. Children are just developing their individual traits and characteristics and it is up to you, as practitioners, to help them to become the individuals they are.

Children will learn to express their thoughts, needs and desires in their own way that is understandable to others. The richness of your personality will impact positively on each child. For example, we all have different levels of liveliness, bounciness, enthusiasm, calmness, and many other different attributes. All these qualities are an enriching experience for children as they grow and develop, to bring out their own inherent character traits. Different moods and interactions are required at different times of the child's day, for example, calmness at sleep time, enthusiasm when looking for mini-beasts, fun when playing rough and tumble.

- **Be an excellent role model to other staff and parents;** for example say good morning with a big smile, 'thank you', and 'how are you today' etc.

Demonstrate polite behavior, such as saying 'pardon me' after burping, thanking a child for giving you a toy, using phrases such as, 'would you like to...go to the toilet?' rather than giving children instructions. Ask children to do things rather than tell them, and use a softer way to lead them into doing things, such as 'let's all go and look for treasure in the garden', 'let's all tidy the house shall we?' They will imitate this interaction with others.

- **Have fun together!** Relax and go with the flow to make the best of the moments children find entertaining. It may be just making funny noises, moving in an amusing way, swinging them upside down or picking up on their funny antics. What you are doing is deepening your relationship with the child through special shared moments. These are magical social interactions that help children to understand humour, and a vital spirited element of human communication.

■ **Connect with babies and toddlers** by copying their noises and facial expressions; by doing so you are expressing pleasure in their company by acknowledging and valuing their unique ways of communicating.

■ **Share children's joy, excitement and achievements** as they make new discoveries and do something for the first time. This applies to all learning achievements; it builds confidence and self-esteem and will be absorbed into their being for them to imitate when others do the same. Also notice and acknowledge when children use new social gestures such as waving 'goodbye', clapping or shaking their head, and any 'signs' they may give for 'nappy', 'milk' etc.

■ **Help children to play together and to make friends.** Children need support to join a group, 'include' others in their games, and play cooperatively.

'Children will take time to learn the rules of interaction such as turn taking and eye contact, but there are activities you can incorporate into your play which will help children understand these rules.' (website: icommunicatetherapy.com, 2017)

Be sensitive to children feeling left out, and approach a group to help them include a child. Also be aware of the overly bossy leaders who may need some help tempering their instructions and expectations.

Join in and model role play, particularly with younger children so they hear and see the etiquette in a shop or with a hairdresser.

■ **Have clear expectations for behaviour** in your setting, such as 'no shoes on the soft play', 'bikes and balls outside', 'tidy up time' when the music comes on, so that children understand what to do.

3. Create the best environment!

■ **Make your setting a welcoming, relaxed and fun place to be.** Think about the entrance area and how it appeals to parents and small children, with relaxing decor, soft furnishings, wall displays, information and toys. Review your playrooms through the eyes of a baby, toddler and young child. Do they have exciting resources, familiar resources and places to relax, be alone, or to chat with a friend?

■ **Plan a variety of role play scenarios.** This gives children places to be social and to try out different social etiquette, such as shop play, home play or a doctor's surgery. Have telephones in these places to support social communication development.

- **Dance and sing every day!** Enjoy songs and music together, both planned and spontaneous, which are natural social experiences where everyone joins in together. Sing as you tidy up, sing at the water tray and make it part of your everyday environment. These enjoyable group experiences are important ways for children to learn language, through rhymes, rhythm and movement.

- **Have communication friendly spaces** (Jarman 2009), where children feel comfortable to chat with adults and friends. Children need to be relaxed and feel confident to chat to you and each other. Calm and cosy places are conducive to talking and thinking. Use tents, drapes, and corners with baskets, soft toys and cushions.

Light has an impact on mood, thinking and learning. Light, airy, spacious areas make us feel positive and energised; cluttered and dark spaces can make us feel overwhelmed and confused. But we all have times when we prefer a duller light to calm us, or a brighter light to liven us up. Children also really enjoy dark spaces and small spaces where they can play and imagine in secret. Using torches and coloured lights can be inviting too. Lamps create a softer light, and can brighten a dark corner.

4. Work with parents

Speak with parents about the importance of chatting to their children as much as possible during everyday routines such as bath-time, getting dressed and meal times. Emphasise the importance of uninterrupted quality time to play and interact every single day, with no TV on, and no phone in hand. Sheridan (2008) highlights the importance of *'creating distraction-free time for interaction with infants.'*

Model how you interact calmly and respectfully with their child when the parent is there. Talk to parents about the friends their child plays with in the setting, and find out about their friends at home or in other settings. Some children show more confidence in another setting, and may chat more, so it is important to find out why.

Discuss how the child is developing their social skills in the setting, giving positive examples of what you have seen them doing and heard them saying.

5. Support children who are learning EAL

It can be very tiring to be in an unfamiliar language environment. (Primary National Strategy, 2007) Children who are being exposed to a completely new language will often stand back and watch, rather than get stuck in to all activities straight away. It is best to just be there with the child as they are absorbing this totally new and unfamiliar environment, reassuring them and helping them feel at ease. Gradually

help them to make small steps towards joining the play, using information gained from home about what they enjoy.

Find out the social norms in each child's culture so that you understand why they use certain non-verbal communication. An example of a cultural difference is the use of eye contact in Japanese societies in comparison to western countries. *'Japanese individuals exhibit less eye contact than do individuals from Western European or North American cultures.'* (Akechi et al, 2013)

It is important to be aware that some cultures have different attitudes towards play. Roopnarine (2010) found that *'Parents in western technologically developed societies were more likely to embrace play as important for children's cognitive and social development and to see themselves as play partners to children'*. She found that in more traditional non-western societies, parents do not consider play to be of great importance; they consider play to be simply something that children do, that parents themselves do not get involved in. This means that some children may feel uncomfortable with adults playing with them if they are not used to it, and so may take time to adjust to their new learning environment.

6. Provide extra support for children with difficulties

You may have some children in your setting who find one or two social communication skills a bit trickier than other children of the same age. For example, you might have a child who has difficulty joining in with other children so they need some encouragement and support. Alternatively,

you might have a child in reception who continues to really struggle to take turns and share.

Think about the specific skills that the individual children struggle with. Look back at the **'Play and Interact'** section in this chapter as well as the **'Get Active!'** activities to follow, and pick out some key strategies and activities that are the most relevant to the children. For children who just need that little bit of extra support, it is a great idea to carry out these activities in a small group with one or two other children, perhaps inviting quieter children to join a child who is shy. Giving the children the opportunities to see good models of the skills that they find difficult can be really powerful, particularly in this small group situation.

Other children in your setting may have more pronounced social communication difficulties. For example, they may:

- appear to have no interest in communicating with others
- play alone for all or most of the time
- appear to be 'in their own little world'
- have inappropriate eye contact with others, for example, too much eye contact, blank stares, or no eye contact at all
- only relate to people to have their needs met
- interact only on their own terms
- be passive or aggressive with others
  (Elks and McLachlan, 2015)

We want to teach these children that interacting with other people is fun!

Involve these children in small group activities that draw on their interests. Support them to turn-take with you or just one other child who is able to take turns easily. Start by having very short turns, for example, putting a car down a ramp, or putting a marble down the marble run. Play other games such as throwing and catching, or rolling a ball between you, which mimics a to and fro conversation.

If you are very concerned about a child in your setting because they appear to have very little interest in interacting with anyone else, speak to their parents about how the child is at home. It would be appropriate to recommend a visit to the GP to discuss this if the parent also has concerns.

Autism Spectrum Condition

'Autism is a lifelong, developmental disability that affects how a person communicates with and relates to other people and how they experience the world around them'. (www.autism.org.uk, 2017)

Although the exact figures are not known, The National Autistic Society report that more than 1 in 100 people in the UK have autism (www.autism.org.uk, 2017). There will also be many other people who are not diagnosed.

No two people with autism are the same; some children with autism will need a higher level of adult support than others. However, to be diagnosed with autism spectrum condition, a person is recognised to have difficulties in three main areas, known as the triad of impairments (Gould and Wing, 1979), these are:

- social relationships
- social communication
- imagination

The way you support a child with autism spectrum condition will be unique to that child. A strong relationship with parents is essential! Making sure that all staff are confident in how to support a child on the autism spectrum will involve meetings with parents and other professionals involved, for example, a speech and language therapist, or an occupational therapist.

Case study: Mikale, 3 years 2 months   PART 2
On page 32, there are some details about Mikale.

Nursery staff had initial concerns about Mikale's social communication skills for a number of reasons. Mikale would always take himself away from the other children. If they came near him or tried to communicate with him he had been seen to make a growling noise. Mikale likes to carry a toy car with him at all times and becomes very distressed when he is not able to do this (e.g. when washing his hands).

Mikale's key person, Jeanna, discussed her concerns with Mikale's mum. His mum reported that Mikale also prefers to be alone at home. She also explained that Mikale will sit for hours with a single toy car, watching the wheels spin as he pushes the car back and forth. She said that tasks, such as washing Mikale and getting him to eat, are very challenging at home. Mum decided that she would book an appointment with Mikale's GP to discuss the concerns.

The GP referred Mikale to the Child Development Centre for a multi-disciplinary assessment. After several months on the waiting list, Mikale was offered an assessment with a paediatrician and several other professionals including a speech and language therapist.

Following this assessment process, Mikale was diagnosed with Autism Spectrum Condition. Parents were provided with an information pack about autism which they shared with the nursery staff. Mikale's mum has also been attending a parent support group to help her support Mikale at home.

Mikale now attends Speech and Language Therapy group sessions at the Child Development Centre and the nursery staff are using the strategies suggested on the paediatrician's report to support Mikale in nursery.

Get active!

Activity 1: Peek-a-boo! (from birth to toddlers!)

Why? Hiding behind things and then popping your head out and saying 'peekaboo' is a sociable, simple and fun activity to do with babies and young toddlers. It supports eye tracking and eye contact and develops a sense of fun.

Resources: You can play Peek-a-boo without any resources at all, such as your hands covering your eyes, a scarf or a blanket, or just around the furniture!

How? Simply hide your face behind your hands, a blanket or whatever else you have to hand. Pop your head out and in view of the child and say "peekaboo!"

Helpful hint: Use your voice in interesting and exciting ways! Say 'Boo' or 'I see you' for a change.

Activity 2: Who's looking? (ball game)

Why? This activity encourages eye contact and using each other's names.

Resources: A selection of balls that the children are likely to want to get their hands on.
For example: squishy balls, tactile sensory balls, flashing balls, koosh balls, balls with glitter inside.

How? A small group of no more than 5 children
- All sit in a circle
- The adult chooses one of the exciting balls
- Explain that you will roll the ball to someone who is looking at you
- Roll the ball to a child who makes eye contact with you
- Then encourage the child who has the ball to look around the circle and roll to someone who is looking at them
- When everyone has had a turn at catching the ball and rolling it ask them to choose another ball

Pass the ball in different ways, for example:
- Rolling the ball
- Bouncing the ball
- Turning around before rolling the ball
- Counting to three and then rolling the ball
- Get inventive and think of other fun ways to pass the ball around!

Helpful hint: Encourage them to say the name of the child they are passing the ball to.

Activity 3: Who is under the blanket? (the children take turns to guess who is under the blanket)

Why? This activity encourages children to interact with others in a fun way, to really look at each other to see who is missing and to use each other's names.

Resources: A blanket big enough for a child, or 2 children to hide underneath!

How? Small group, no more than 8 children
- Everyone sits in a circle
- Ask the children to look at everyone and go round and say everyone's name, they must try and remember who is there!
- Place the blanket on the floor in the middle of the circle
- If possible, use an adult to demonstrate first
- Ask the adult to turn around or just step outside the room
- Explain to the children that someone is going to hide under the blanket

- Ask who would like to hide under then blanket
- When the child is hidden under the blanket, bring the adult back in the room
- The adult has to guess who is hiding
- When the adult has guessed, lift the blanket up to reveal who is underneath
- Then ask who else would like to guess and they either turn around or step outside the room with the other adult.

Helpful hint: Remind the children that they should not tell the person who is guessing who is under the blanket! This can be very tricky for some young children – they find it very challenging to keep secrets! Also 2 children could hide under the blanket if the group is larger. They could make funny noises, like animals to help the person guess!

Encourage the children to sit back in the same place in the circle after hiding under the blanket. This way, it will make it easier for the other children to guess who is missing from the circle. Or if they find it too easy, let everyone move around, this will keep it active!

Activity 4: Microphone game

Why? This is a turn-taking game that helps children understand about taking turns in conversations.

Resources: A toy microphone. If you do not have a toy microphone, you can use an item that resembles a microphone (a hairbrush) or a real microphone!

How? Small group, no more than 6 children
- Show the children the microphone and explain this is the microphone game
- Explain that you walk around the circle when you have the microphone
- First tell the children to think about their favourite animal

- Then start off by walking around the inside of the circle and saying into the microphone 'I like dogs' (or any other animal)
- Then pass the microphone to an adult who does the same and says 'I like elephants'
- Then pass the microphone to a child and let them share their favourite animal with the group
- Children pass the microphone to someone else (or pass around the circle)
- Then change the topic, for example, favourite colour, food, drink or toy.

Helpful hint: Make the sentence longer to extend talking. Use phrases like, 'my favourite toy is my blue rabbit', 'I love going swimming'.

Activity 5: Dancing!

Why? Dancing is a feel-good activity that is social and fun! Children are also watching you and listening to you, if you say what you do when you do it. You don't always have to talk, just move!

Resources: Lively music with a good beat.

How? Large group or with one child!
Play music and jig about.
Encourage children to clap, wave their arms from one side to another, wiggle their hips, bend their knees, lift their knees, point their toes onto floor, do the same with heels, twirl, and jump!
Then just do free dancing to the music, commenting on their moves such as, 'lovely twirling Nina!' or 'I like your wiggly hips Imran!'

Helpful hint: Ask children to hold hands with someone as they dance, (2s or 3s), to have fun together.

Activity 6: Chalk drawing

Why? All about me chalk drawings increase a child's self-awareness, which helps them with their social communication with others.

Resources: An outdoor space with a surface suitable for drawing on with chalk, chunky chalks in a range of colours.

How?
- Encourage the children to draw themselves or a friend
- Talk with them about what they have drawn ('Ooh yes, you've done your long brown hair')
- Encourage them to draw something that they like.

Helpful hint: With younger children you could draw around their body, either on the ground or on a wall. Ask them to add eyes, nose, hair etc. and chat about their different features.

Get active!

Activity 7: Corners

Why? This is a versatile and sociable game that can be organised in many ways to enable children to play together, have fun and work things out.

Resources: A cone or marker in the centre of the room.

How? Organise large groups into 3/4 smaller groups and each go to an edge of the area, use corners if 4 groups.
- give each group a name according to what you want to emphasise, for example, colours, shapes or numbers
- give each group an activity to do in turn, such as run, skip, jump, or dance
- they do the activity in a line around the cone in the centre, following each other, all moving together
- a variation is to give each group a name like 'the dancing group', 'the hopping group' the walking backwards group, and they move accordingly
- children move round to a different corner and change their activity.

Helpful hint: Once children have got used to the game, they can decide on their own group identity, and others can guess it by the way they move, for example, they can choose to move like different animals.
Adapt for smaller group by using 3 corners and 2 children in each corner.

Activity 8: Bubbles

Why? Children of all ages love bubbles, it is a very sociable activity to share a fun time together.

Resources: Bubble machine for young children, bubble mixture (one part washing-up liquid to 4/5 parts water, and few drops of glycerine) and a range of different bubble wands.

How? Just let the bubbles flow from the machine and watch the children's excitement as they try to catch them! Let older children use the wands to create their own bubbles; some children will make the bubbles and others will chase them.

Helpful hint: For older children, and an exciting experience, use a hoop and a big container like a tough spot tray, and stand a child in the centre, lift the hoop to create a bubble around the child!

Activity 9: The active 'Hello' song

Why? This is a fun, active and enjoyable way to greet children at each session.

Resources: Enthusiasm!

How? Use your usual 'hello' song and put actions to it.

'Hello Hassan, hello Hassan, hello Hassan and how are you today?'

Or, 'Hello Evie, hello Evie, hello Evie, we're glad you're here today.'

Add a different repetitive action for each child as you sing, for example, clap high in the air, rock from side to side, tap your feet on the floor with hands behind you, wave arms from side to side, sparkle with your fingers by stretching and curling them, roly poly arms down to your toes and back or stretch arms up high then out in front of you. Continue doing the same simple action for the whole song for each child.

Helpful hint: When children are used to this sitting down, progress to standing and do more energetic actions actions such as, jumping, tapping toes alternately on the floor, bending knees and clapping or rocking from one leg to the other with arms outstretched.

Activity 10: Parachute games

Why? This is a fun, sociable activity that can be used in many ways to help children develop listening skills and enjoy being together. You can develop lots of maths understanding too!

Resources: A parachute, different things that are easy to pick up such as bean bags, small balls, quoits, wooden/plastic bricks. Put them all underneath the parachute.

How? Ask specific children to run in and collect 3 green balls, 2 things that are round, 4 beanbags, etc. Choose the action to suit the child's understanding.
Use balls to bounce up and down on the parachute and count how many bounces before they bounce off!

Helpful hint: Continue the game by reversing the instructions to take things back underneath. Children run around the outside and collect the things that have been brought out.

For younger children, use colour, ask children with blue shoes, wearing something red, to run into the middle and back or run across to the other side of the parachute.

Parachute counting game

Resources: Parachute and number necklaces (cards with numbers on the front and with cord to make a necklace).

How?
- Give each child a number necklace to put on
- Give lots of number based instuctions, depending on children's level of understanding, such as:
- Numbers 3 and 5 change places
- Run around the outside if you are less than 7
- Run into the middle if you are more than 5
- Run underneath the parachute if you are one more than 3

Helpful hint: Make sure the 'number necklaces' are safe to wear and run around in.

Activity 11: Duck duck goose

Why? This is a fun, sociable, active game where children interact naturally and enjoy chasing each other.

Resources: Outdoor space or space indoors!

How? A maximum of 8 children sit in a circle with the adult
- One child walks around the outside of the circle tapping children gently on the head saying, 'Duck, duck, duck, duck...goose!'

- The child who is the goose, gets up and chases the other child around the outside of the circle and tries to catch them before they sit down in the goose's place
- The 'goose' is now the child who goes around tapping heads
- They decide themselves when to say 'goose'
- Continue until everyone has had a turn.

Helpful hint: This can be played with younger children who will love to be chased! The adult can be the person chasing until they get the hang of it.

Tables of development

Social Communication

Development of social communication from 0–12 months (Based on Sheridan, 2008)	
Birth	Babies interact with their carers through eye contact, spontaneous or imitative facial gestures and their changing sleep-wakefulness state. Babies prefer social stimuli, coo and make pre-speech lip and tongue movements responsively to parent's or carer's talk.
By one month	Babies maintain and terminate eye-to-eye contact, stop crying when picked up and spoken to, and turn to look at speaker.
By three months	Babies show excitement at the sound of approaching voices, footsteps, running bathwater etc. They vocalise delightedly when spoken to, smile, make eye contact, use hand gestures and take turns to 'talk'. They respond with obvious pleasure to friendly handling, especially when accompanied by playful tickling, child friendly speech and singing.
By six months	Babies recognise carer's facial expressions, such as happy or fearful, and respond selectively to emotional tones of voice, for example, by smiling in response to an enthusiastic happy voice. They delight in rough-and-tumble play, react enthusiastically to repeated games and anticipate the high points in nursery rhymes and songs. They are still friendly with strangers, but occasionally show shyness or slight anxiety when an adult approaches suddenly, especially if their familiar adult is out of sight. They become more reserved with strangers from about 7 months.
By nine months	Babies clearly distinguish strangers from familiar people and require reassurance before accepting their advances; they may cling to the known person and hide their face. They play peek-a-boo, copy hand-clapping, watch a toy being hidden under a cover or cup, and find it.
By 12 months	Infants play pat-a-cake, wave 'good-bye', both on request and spontaneously They enjoy playing with adults.

Development of friendship skills (Based on Sheridan, 2008)	
18 months	Toddler shows awareness of another child's distress.
2 years	Child shows preferences for particular companions and cooperates with a shared play theme like a tea party.
2½ years	Child plays roles like doctor-patient, mother-baby, shopkeeper and customer. They are aware of what is 'pretend', like eating play food, talking to teddies.
3 years	Child talks about friendship, such as 'you are my best friend', 'you are not my friend today'; refers to all playmates as friends; sometimes there is conflict between friends; some children have imaginary friends.

Section 3: Active Understanding

Why is it important?

○ Speech Sounds

○ Talking

● Understanding

○ Social Communication

○ Attention and Listening

'Receptive language is indeed at the heart of all other aspects of language learning.'

'Without this a child's ability to develop social relationships, build spoken language and generally develop as a literate and numerate individual will be seriously affected.' (Hayes, 2016)

This section is all about promoting children's understanding of language, known as receptive language skills. 'Receptive language' refers to a person's ability to understand what someone is saying to them. It involves understanding words, sentences and the meaning of what someone has said. This section refers to both 'understanding' and 'receptive language' interchangeably. However, it is important to remember that when referring to 'understanding' this relates solely to 'understanding language', not understanding in general, for example, ideas, routines or whose turn it is to help with snacks.

Looking at the **Communication Climbing Frame**, in order to **understand** what is being said, the child needs **to listen and pay attention** to the person speaking. This is of course a **social interaction**. So both these skills form a base for **understanding**. However, children may have these fundamental skills and still struggle with understanding the spoken word.

> **Early Learning Goal (expected achievement for children by the end of the EYFS)**
>
> **Understanding:** children follow instructions involving several ideas or actions. They answer 'how' and 'why' questions about their experiences and in response to stories or events.
> **Statutory Framework for the EYFS, 2017**

Take a look at the left hand side of the **Communication Chain** (page 5). You will see that a number of processes are involved in understanding language. In order to fully understand what they hear, a child needs to remember what they have heard for long enough to process and then understand the words and the sentences. They then need to work out the overall meaning of the language.

Understanding comes before **talking** on the **Communication Climbing Frame** as children typically understand far more words than they actually use themselves when talking.

> *'We know that children's receptive language (the words they understand) is more advanced than their expressive language (the words they can say).'*
> (Mooney, 2005)

There is an area in the brain called the Wernicke's area. This is often referred to as the 'receptive language centre' as it is one of the main areas responsible for language comprehension.

This receptive language centre in the brain is located near to the part of the brain that is often referred to as the 'sensory strip'. This is called the parietal lobe and it receives tactile, visual and auditory information. (Simpkins and Simpkins, 2013). This means that it receives information about what we see, hear and feel.

Jaak Panksepp (1998) has studied this area in great depth. His work suggests that, due to the location of the 'receptive language centre' in the brain, humans need auditory, visual, tactile and movement experiences to develop receptive language. This is in addition to social experiences with other people.

With the brain research in mind, offering pre-school children a wide range of active and multisensory experiences every day is therefore a great way to promote receptive language skills.

The ability to understand language is vital; children need to have good receptive language skills before they can use language to express themselves. They need to understand the meaning of words before they can use them appropriately when talking.

Children need to use receptive language skills to:
- understand what others are saying
- follow instructions
- understand and respond to questions
- listen to stories
- play with other children cooperatively
- be a social person

Reflection

Consider the children in your key group and check their levels of understanding against the guidance chart on page 61.

Developmental stages of understanding language

Caroline Bowen has identified the steps that children usually go through in the process of developing receptive language skills. The table on page 61 shows these developmental stages. As with all areas of child development, it is important to remember that all children develop at different rates so the age bands are very flexible.

Case Study: Ada, 3½ years old

Ada responds well to adults, chats confidently and follows instructions at nursery. She responds appropriately to most simple questions. She knows what happens next in books and often retells familiar stories. She also helps younger children with routines like tidying up. Ada enjoys interacting with peers and can often be found in the home corner at nursery.

Ada's receptive language skills are typical for her age.

Case Study: Joudi, 4 years 6 months   PART 1

Joudi has difficulties following what the teacher asks her to do in reception. Joudi's teacher says that Joudi often looks blankly when she is given an instruction or asked a question.

Joudi is able to answer very simple questions, for example, 'what's that?', however when asked a 'where question' or a 'who question', Joudi often looks blankly back at the adult, or says something unrelated to the question.

Staff have noticed that Joudi will often copy other children when she is not sure what to do.

Joudi's receptive language skills are delayed for her age.

There is more information about the steps that staff have taken to support Joudi in reception.
See Case study: Joudi PART 2 page 52

See Case study: Joudi PART 2 page 52

The importance of books

There is research to suggest that sharing books with pre-school children can promote their understanding of language (Wasik and Bond, 2001).

Sharing books with young children supports their receptive language skills for a number of reasons.

- It gives them the opportunity to encounter vocabulary that they may not necessarily hear in everyday conversations. (Wasik and Bond, 2001)

- Children's books are very visual and full of colourful pictures that children are usually drawn to. When adults read the words or talk about the pictures while pointing to them, the pictures help the children to understand the words. This supports receptive language development.

- The words and pictures in books are always there to come back to *'unlike speech, which 'disappears'*

as soon as we finish talking' (Pepper and Weitzman, 2004). The permanence of the words and pictures in books makes it easier for children to learn new words.

Wasik and Bond (2001) also found that when the sharing of books is made more active with the use of props, children are very interested in the props, which makes it easier for them to learn the names of the items.

Difficulties with understanding

Problems with understanding the spoken word create a huge barrier to learning. Children find it hard to respond to requests, questions and conversations, and struggle to interact appropriately with other children of their age.

Children who struggle to understand language are sometimes mistaken for misbehaving because they may not do what is expected of them. They may appear to ignore requests and guidance because they haven't actually understood the language used. As they get older, children with receptive language difficulties often use a range of clever strategies to cope in their environment. These strategies will mask their difficulties with understanding. For this reason, it can be tricky to spot receptive language problems.

> *'They may look blank, pull faces, smile or giggle, cry or sulk, hide or hit out. They may carry on doing the same thing although you think you've clearly told them to stop, or they may do the opposite of what you say...'*
> (McMinn, 2006)

Some children may watch and copy the actions of their peers when group instructions are given, so they appear to understand. Their difficulties are easily masked, so they may be overlooked and not receive the help they need.

Since some children are adept at hiding their difficulties in understanding spoken language, it is crucial that you promote receptive language clearly with all children.

Identifying difficulties using Information-Carrying Words (ICW)

Knowing about 'information-carrying words' (ICW) helps you to work out how much language a child actually understands. Information-carrying words are *'the words in a sentence that the child must understand in order to carry out an instruction'.* (Halliwell, 2003)

For example, a child is presented with a banana, an apple and an orange. The adult asks, 'where is the banana', BANANA is the ICW that enables the child to answer the question and point to the right fruit. If there was only a banana available, and the child was asked the same question, banana would not

be an ICW because it is the only option and the child doesn't need to know the word to carry out the task.

Understanding ICWs helps you to interact with children at the right level and adapt your language according to the age of the child. Also, when using ICW as a tool to see how much a child understands, it is important to avoid the use of gestures, for example, pointing to items and other forms of non-verbal communication such as eye pointing.

A child's ability to follow instructions develops over time as their understanding improves. A one year old child can usually follow an instruction with one ICW. For example, if a child is playing with a doll, and you say, 'feed the baby', the child needs to understand 'FEED' as the 'baby' is already part of the understood context.

By age 2, children can usually follow instructions containing two ICWs. If you're playing with a toy farm and you ask the child to 'make the cow run', (when there are a few other animals to choose from) this is a 2 ICW level instruction, with COW and RUN as the ICWs.

By age 3, children should be able to follow instructions that contain three pieces of information. For example, 'can you make the big dog jump?' (when big and small versions of various animals are in sight).

By the time a child is 4, it is expected that they can follow instructions that require them to understand four pieces of information.

The adult role

1. Take an active approach

Use the body to learn words and phrases. So much of our vocabulary is active, and as we know, verbs are 'doing' words. Children can 'jump' and 'splash' in the puddles, they can 'hop', 'climb', 'balance', and 'walk'. They will do these things 'quickly' or 'slowly', 'quietly' or 'loudly', they will reach 'high' or 'low' so use this as an opportunity to help them learn adverbs. They learn about their body parts as 'bend their knees', 'wiggle their hips', and 'wave their hands', so they are learning nouns.

Dance and imaginative movement sessions can introduce a wide vocabulary relating to body movements, for example, 'swirling' around like smoke, 'whizzing around' and 'leaping into the air' like fireworks, 'prowling' like a lion. By 'doing' the word, it becomes visual, real and meaningful.

It is natural for us to use movement and gesture to help children to understand what we say. From an early age we point to things and name them, we say 'let's go to the ......' as we 'go'

somewhere. We ask toddlers to 'fetch a book', 'throw the ball', or 'play in the garden'. It is a fun and exciting way for young children to naturally learn language. They will enjoy following instructions to 'throw the beanbags at the cone',' jump in the hoop', 'run around the tree', and 'climb up the ladder'. Also, by seeing someone else do a physical activity, they can copy them and begin to connect the words with the actions.

2. Play and Interact

As a key person, you play a central role in helping children to understand language. As you spend the most time with the child, you get to know what things they can understand and what their early babbles and language mean. You can help them understand things as you play with them and chat each day.

When playing and interacting with the children there are some simple strategies that you can use to help them develop their understanding of language. Many of these you will do naturally as an early years practitioner.

- **Sing songs spontaneously** at a range of activities as well as at a group time. **(See Get Active!)**. Singing songs with young children has a wide range of benefits. There is research to suggest that singing with children supports receptive language development (Blythe, 2011). The repetitive nature of songs provides children with good models of language that they can hear over and over again. Songs with actions are great as the actions help the children to understand what is being said. Also, children can have fun and get involved in a no pressured situation. (*Principle 1:* Children need to hear many words often)

- **Speak slowly and pause** to give children time to respond. There is a lot for children to process in a conversation. Look at the **Communication Chain** on page 5. Children need time to process what they have heard to formulate their thoughts and then find the words to speak. Children will follow your example, by taking time to answer and slowing their speech down too.

- **Model language** by naming what they are handling, or playing with children to link the spoken word with the object. Similarly, name the actions children do; if the child is in the toy kitchen playing with a tea set, say, 'pouring' as they pretend to pour tea. You can do this during everyday activities too such as 'wash wash, wash' when supporting a child to wash their hands.

  This is important because children need to hear a word whilst seeing the item (or action) several times before they will use the word confidently themselves. (*Principle 1:* Children need to hear many words often)

- **Comment more**. It is natural to ask questions, however questions do not support receptive language in the same way as comments do. For every question that you ask, try and make at least four comments. For example, 'What's that?', 'Wow, you're building! Oooh a red brick; that is very high! One, two, three, Crash!'

- **Let there be silence!** Children need time to process the words that they are hearing. They may not respond straight away for various reasons; they may be focusing on their play, just not want to speak or they may be thinking about what you have said.

- **Use natural gestures when talking**. This will help children to understand what you are saying. For example, when asking a child to flush the toilet, mime flushing a toilet yourself. Or when asking a child to wash his hands, mime washing your hands.

- **Use a signing support system**. There are several sign support systems such as Signalong or Makaton that can be used to support the children in your setting to understand the words you say.

'Signing and meaningful gestures are highly recommended to help children's understanding and use of communication'. (Nash, Lowe, Leah, 2013.

The idea is that you make the sign whilst saying the words, rather than replacing words with signs. If a child sees you make a sign whilst saying a word that they do not yet understand, the sign will help them to understand what the word means. If you are new to signing, it is recommended that you learn a small number of the most important signs, for example, nappy, milk, toilet, finished. (www.signalong.org.uk)

- **Be consistent** in the language you all use. For example, with a baby, if waving 'goodbye', try not to mix a number of similar words such as 'bye' 'ta ta' 'cheerio'. Check what they use at home.

- **Use other visual aids**. Sometimes, it can help to use pictures, photographs or toys to help children understand what you are saying, all depending on the context.

- **Use books**, they are an ideal way of helping children to connect spoken words and pictures. Early baby books focus mainly on nouns, things, people and animals. Then they develop into people, animals and other characters doing things, so children begin to understand and consolidate verbs. Most practitioners point to things in the book and comment, 'there is the red tractor' or ask, 'where is the...mouse?' so the child gets to understand the words.

Read the child's responses. If you can tell that the child has not understood what you have said to them, Simplify your language, break down instructions into smaller chunks, Show the child what you mean! Give options, for example, carrots, sweetcorn and peas. Show each vegetable when you name it. Or you might ask, 'Shall we use glue or sellotape?' This way, the child hears the name and starts to make the link between the word and the item.

Reflection

Read the two examples of interactions between an adult and a child and think about the differences in communication from the adult.

Example 1
Adult 1: 'What have you got?'
*Child: *Looks at adult**
Adult 1: 'What is it?'
*Child: *Continues to play and does not look up at adult**
Adult 1: 'Where does that go?'
*Child: *Does not respond verbally and continues to play**

Example 2
Adult 2: 'It's a train!'
*Child: *Looks at adult and then gives adult a toy train**
*Adult 2: 'Choo choo' *train gesture with arms**
*Child: 'Choo choo' *train gesture with arms**
Adult 2:'Wow, fast train!'
*Child: *Looks at adult and nods and then makes train go even faster**
Adult: 'Through the tunnel!' 'Uh oh...crash!'
*Child: 'Uh oh' *laughs**

Adult 1 asks question after question.
Adult 2 is commenting on the child's play.

You can see that the child in the second interaction is far more responsive to what the adult is saying.

Adult 2 is supporting the child's understanding of language by:
- naming items for the child, 'It's a train'. Naming items and actions is a great way to teach children new words. Name the item when the child is looking at it, or name the action when the child is doing it
- keeping her language simple
- using an arm gesture when saying 'choo choo' by using signs/hand gestures to accompany the words, it is easier for children to learn the meaning of the word

letting the child lead the play and the interaction, by providing the child with a running commentary, the adult is showing a genuine interest in the activity so the child is more likely to respond.

As adults, we naturally ask questions to other adults because it is one way we keep the conversation flowing. However when communicating with young children, and promoting receptive language, it is important to limit questions and simply comment instead.

3. Create the best environment!

You can organise the environment in ways that promote understanding and language development. It is important, however, to consider a host of other factors when planning your environment too, such as providing for a wide range of intelligences (Gardner 1999), children's interests and common schemas.

- **Create distinct activity and storage areas.**
  'Arrange your environment to create distinct activity zones including quiet areas and messy areas.' (oxfordshire.gov.uk, 2008)

  Clearly defined areas for activities make it easier for a child to focus on the resources, and to know what to expect from the area. Also, it is often easier to relate the language in a specific area to the resources and activity, and so make it easier for the child to learn words and understand language used. This supports the principles that spur language learning:
  Principle 1: Children need to hear many words often
  Principle 4: Words are learned when meanings are made clear. However, within these distinct areas, children should be able to move resources from one area to another to develop their play. For example, if they need blocks to add to their train track for buildings and bridges, and people to add to the scene, they need to know where to find them.

  Outdoors, play areas are usually more fluid and less defined, although there are likely to be specific areas for sand play, the play house and physical play equipment, for example. Again, it is important that children are able to move resources from one place to another to develop their play, so they need to know where to find them. For example, the tyres are behind the play house or the gardening tools are on the shelves in the storage shed.

- **Label areas and equipment with words and pictures or photos.** This enables children to identify play areas, know where to find resources and to tidy up!

■ **Provide multi-sensory experiences**. Children learn through doing. Multi-sensory experiences are meaningful and memorable and this is vital to help children understand and remember language. Slime will be 'wet' and 'slimy', then goop will 'drip', playdough will be 'soft' and 'stretch'. So these sensory activities help them understand the meaning of these words through hands-on experiences.

■ **Use visual timetables**. Visual timetables use pictures to show the children what will be happening throughout the day, and in what order.

Having pictures to refer to helps children to understand what they will be doing next, and to see a pattern to the day. They can see what they have done and refer back to these pictures at any time. They will become familiar with the daily routine and soon know what to expect. A visual timetable also helps children to begin to understand the concept of time, for example, words such as 'after', 'next', 'later'.

4. Work with parents

'Parents are the most influential people in children's lives'. (Bray in Kersner and Wright, 2012)

'Children's development of language is often directly related to the amount of time that parents spend talking to them, and the same growth is not experienced by hearing people talk on television.' (Ray, 2016)

Model positive interactions with children in front of parents. It is so important that parents are playing and interacting with their children in a positive way. As early years practitioners, you are great people to inspire parents and give them ideas about activities and games that they could try at home. Tell parents about an activity that their child really enjoyed that day and what that activity actually involved. For example, 'Tommy loved playing with the water today; we were pouring and dripping water from cups. He really liked it when we were pouring the water from up high.' This way, parents may attempt to replicate the activities at home. You could show them photographs of them absorbed in their play.

Encourage parents to have 'story time' every day with their child. Perhaps have a book library and 'Storysacks' to borrow.

Communicate with parents! Let parents know how important it is to talk to their children, to have 'phone free' times, and to reduce TV hours. Put posters up in the entrance area to highlight key messages. Research shows that some parents don't fully understand the importance of talking to their children during uninterrupted, distraction-free situations. (The National Literacy Trust, 2011; Spooner and Woodcock, 2013)

5. Support children who are learning EAL

'Additional visual support is vital for children learning English and using illustration and artefacts will also support and enhance the learning experiences of their monolingual peers.'
(Primary National Strategy, 2007)

Use all of the strategies listed in the 'Adult role: Play and Interact' section on pages 47-48.

Do all of the following when communicating with children with limited knowledge of English:
- ✓ name the things that the child is looking at
- ✓ comment more and question less
- ✓ use very simple language
- ✓ use gestures and visuals to support what you say
- ✓ encourage interaction with peers; they learn a lot from other children, as all children usually have a natural incentive to join in play

Emphasise the home language

'For children whose home language is not English, providers must take reasonable steps to provide opportunities for children to develop and use their home language in play and learning, supporting their language development at home.'
(Statutory Framework for the early years foundation stage, 2017)

It is important to encourage children to use their home language so that their thought processes for working things out continue to develop at a good rate. It is crucial to ensure that their communication and learning continues to develop at home where they spend most of their time, and it is essential for helping them to develop spoken English.

'Home language skills are transferable to new languages and strengthen children's understanding of language use.'
(Department for children, schools and families, 2007)

Find out key phrases and words in the child's first language to help connect with them, meet fundamental needs and develop a relationship.

6. Provide extra support for children with difficulties

Use the same strategies already outlined to help children to understand meaning and language.

Simplify instructions, tell the child again on a one to one basis. For example, if you tell the group "everyone it's time to wash your hands", say to the child who struggles to understand "Alex, wash hands" when face to face with the child and while doing a washing hands action.

Keep your language simple. Lathey and Blakey (2013) recommend that you use language that is just slightly more advanced than the language the child uses and use lots of repetition.

Use a sign support system. Signing can be particularly powerful when used with children who are struggling to understand language.

Use other visuals such as pictures and photographs. Key photographs, pictures and symbols could be printed on cards and then kept on a lanyard so that they can be used with these children whenever required. Showing children symbols whilst also saying words can be really beneficial in terms of helping children to understand the meaning of that word.

There are several electronic symbol creating programs that are available commercially, for example, 'Boardmaker' and 'Communicate in print'. These tools enable you to type in any word and obtain a range of symbols that you can use to represent that word. For more information visit www.widgit.com.

Talk about things as they happen. Emphasise the 'here and now' as this is meaningful and concrete. Many pre-school children have difficulties understanding abstract concepts such as 'later' or 'tomorrow'.

Avoid using ambiguous, abstract and non-literal language, as this is very confusing for young children who are struggling to understand language. Examples of non-literal phrases include: 'It's a piece of cake', 'You're on the ball today', 'Are you feeling under the weather?'

Provide a simple running commentary as you follow the child's lead in play, so that they connect their actions with words. For example, 'the man is climbing the ladder, he is on the roof, the cat is on the roof too'.

Notice any difficulties with attention and listening. Children with receptive language difficulties may also present attention and listening difficulties. This is unsurprising, because when children don't understand what is being said to them, they may switch off and stop listening. If this is the case, refer back to Section 1: Attention and listening.

Case study: Joudi, 4 years 6 months   PART 2
Joudi was introduced earlier in this chapter (see page 45).

Joudi has difficulties with understanding the language used by others in her reception class. For example, she often looks blank when she is given an instruction or asked a question.

All staff in Joudi's class have been working hard to reduce the number of questions they ask Joudi, and comment more instead. When they ask her to do something, they simplify their language so that the instructions are easier for her to understand.

One of the early years practitioners is trained in Signalong and she has taught the other practitioners a selection of key signs. They have all been using these signs when talking to Joudi.

Staff have noticed that Joudi responds really well to the Signalong signs. Since staff have used simpler language, this has had a really positive impact on Joudi. Now her teacher feels that she is able to understand most of what staff members say to her.

Get active!

Activity 1: Spontaneous singing!

Why? Most children love action rhymes. Children learn to put actions to words and if the song is related to the activity, it is in context and easier to relate to. Children understand and learn phrases and vocabulary from songs as they are repetitive and they hear them often.

Resources: Any area in the room or outdoors! The words of the rhymes can be found on the internet if you search the title.

How? Here are some ideas, although there are many more:
Water play: 5 little ducks, 5 speckled frogs, Row, row, row your boat, 1, 2, 3, 4, 5, once I caught a fish alive.
Home area: Polly put the kettle on, I'm a little teapot, Rock-a-Bye baby, Miss Polly had a dolly, Pat a cake, Ten in the bed.
Cars, garage, vehicles: The wheels on the bus.
Farm: Little Bo Peep, Old McDonald had a farm, Baa Baa black sheep.
Zoo: Mud, mud, glorious mud! 5 little monkeys,
Outdoors: See-saw Margery daw, Wiggly Woo, 5 green speckled frogs.

Helpful hint: MAKE UP YOUR OWN RHYMES!
Choo Choo, Choo Choo, Choo Choo Choo Choo train!
Here it comes, round and round, round and round again!
People wave, off we go, off to places we don't know,
Home we come, had some fun Choo Choo Choo train!

Get active!

Activity 2: Here we go round the mulberry bush

Why? This is a fun and sociable way to understand action phrases.

Resources: You, the practitioner! This can be done with as few as 2 children and also in a large group.

How? Join hands and sing the song together
Here we go round the mulberry bush, the mulberry bush the mulberry bush
Here we go round the mulberry bush on a cold and frosty morning!
This is the ways we:
clap our hands, clap our hands, clap our hands,
This is the way we clap our hands on a cold and frosty morning!

Continue with a range of actions such as:

Brush our hair, jump about, touch our nose (toes, etc), turn around, pat our tummy, bend our knees, stand on one leg, brush our teeth, stamp our feet...the list is endless!

Helpful hint: Ask the children to suggest the actions once they have got the idea!

Activity 3: 'We like to jump' song

Why? Children love jumping and doing different actions in songs. They can easily understand the word by relating it to the action.

Resources: Plenty of space.

How? First teach the children the song 'We like to jump' (make up a tune!)
We like to jump, we like to jump. We like to jump, jump, jump, jump, jump!
We like to jump, we like to jump, we like to jump and play!

Change the ending each time to a different verb, for example, run, walk, wave, swim, eat.
Pretend to carry out the each action whilst singing.

Helpful hint: For an added element of fun, sing the song quietly, loudly, quickly or slowly. Children are often motivated by changing these elements when singing a familiar song.

Activity 4: Toy peek-a-boo
(Young children 0-18 months)

Why? Naming the items that the child is looking at is one of the most powerful ways of supporting a young child's understanding.

Resources: A doll, a teddy and a selection of animal soft toys or puppets such as a duck and a rabbit. A draw string bag big enough for the doll, teddy and puppets.

How?
Use an exciting tone of voice to draw your child's attention to your bag of toys.
Put your hand into the bag with an excited facial expression and pull out one item.
As you pull out the item name it, for example, 'teddy!'
Pretend that the character is talking to the child for up to 30 seconds, using very simple language, for example, 'Hello Ahyan, jump, jump, jump!, Bye bye!' (1-3 words at a time)
Put your hand in the bag again with an excited facial expression and pull out another item.
Again name the item as it pops into the child's view.

Helpful hint: Let the children take turns in pulling something out of the bag, and leading the activity.

Activity 5: Find it!

Why? This is a fun, hands-on way to support children's understanding of a wide range of nouns.

Resources: Sandtray, sandpit or soil.

A range of toy animal figures for example, a horse, cow, dog, cat, duck, giraffe or dinosaurs.
A range of plastic toy foods for example, egg, toast, banana, biscuit or apple
A range of real life household items for example, toothbrush, cup, plastic plate.
A range of toy vehicles for example, car, bus, train, tractor.

Note: Ensure that nothing with sharp edges is used.

How? Before you start, hide the items in the sand or soil so that they cannot be seen.
Name an item and encourage the children to look for it.
When a child finds the item, ensure that all children stop, look and listen. Comment on the find!
('Tommy, you found a tractor!')
Put the items on a table or surface as they are found.
Name all the items each time 'Now we have...a horse...a car...a toothbrush...a dinosaur!'

Note: The number of children that can play this game at any one time depends on the size of your sandtray, sandpit or soil area.

Helpful hint: Children can re-hide the items for other children to find or to play again; they can say 'I found a banana!'

For babies, hide a number of items under a blanket, or newspaper. As the child finds the items, simply name the item ('Ooooh teddy, teddy!')

Activity 6: 'Do the action' game!

Why? This is a fun and active way to help children understand 'doing words'.

Resources: Plenty of space.

How? Explain to the children that when you say 'FREEZE', they have to stand still and listen.
Say an 'action' and encourage the children to carry out the action. For example, 'run', 'crawl'.
After a short time, (about 15 seconds) call 'FREEZE' and wait until all children have stopped the action and are looking at you.
Name the next action verb, and so on.

Verb list: jump, walk, crawl, wave, sleep, run, laugh, cry, dance, wiggle, sing, eat, slide, clap, hop, roll, wobble etc.

Helpful hint: For children who struggle with this, go through the verb list on a one to one basis before playing the game with a group.

Get active!

Activity 7: Make a silly pizza

Why? This is a fun way to help children to understand and follow instructions. Concepts, such as big and small, can be introduced here for the children who are able to follow the more simple instructions.

Resources:
Large red cardboard circles (for the base of the silly pizzas, one per child).
Smaller red circles (for the base of smaller silly pizzas, one per child).
A selection of small pictures of foods and non-food items
Puppet.

How? Prepare a silly pizza beforehand and show the children your silly pizza
Present the children with their large red cardboard circles (one per child)
Have various pictures of foods and also of other things, for example, pictures of a phone, blanket, toothbrush, fork, grass, flower etc.
Tell the children what to put on their pizza. Start with just asking them to add one thing to their pizza, perhaps chocolate!
Name two more items for the children to add to their pizza, perhaps banana and shoes!

For the children who are able to add two items to the pizza without difficulty, present them with a smaller pizza base in

addition to their larger pizza. Then give instructions such as: put the fork on the little pizza, put the pencil on the big pizza.

Helpful hint: Puppets can be used to add an extra element of fun to this activity. The puppet can give the instructions to the children, and pretend that he/she likes all sorts of bizarre combinations of pizza toppings!

Activity 8: Help Teddy

Why? This is a fun way to help children to understand and learn words and phrases and follow simple instructions.

Resources: Teddy and dolly. A selection of clothes that fit the teddy bear and the dolly, a toy brush.

How? Explain to the children that Teddy is feeling poorly today. Say 'poor Teddy'.
Say that you are all going to help Teddy to feel better. Demonstrate stroking Teddy.
Show the children that you also have a brush, and demonstrate brushing Teddy.

Then give the children instructions that require them to stroke or brush various body parts, such as ears, tummy, back, feet.

Examples of instructions:
Brush Teddy's ears
Stroke Teddy's back
Stroke Teddy's tummy
Feed Teddy

Helpful hint: If the children are able to follow the instructions to help Teddy, you could introduce a second character, for example a doll or a soft toy dog. Then alternate instructions between the characters 'brush dolly's hair', 'stroke Teddy's back'.

Activity 9: Blowing bubbles

Why? Children love bubbles! So this activity is a motivating way to help children to understand prepositions (e.g. on, in, under).

Resources: A pot of bubbles. A chair and table, use your outdoor areas, such as a tunnel, climbing frame.

How? Tell the children that we can blow bubbles in lots of different places.
Demonstrate blowing bubbles 'up' and 'down'.
Then, when the children take a turn, give them an instruction (without pointing) 'blow bubbles up', or 'blow bubbles down'
Use the table and demonstrate again. Show the children that we can blow the bubbles **on** the table or **under** the table
Ask children to:
'Blow bubbles **on** the table/ **under** the table/**through** the fence/ **through** the tunnel/**under** the chair and in various other places in your garden.

Helpful hint: Some children struggle to physically blow bubbles using a standard bubble wand, encourage them to wave it in the air.

Helpful hint: If the children are struggling to understand 'on' and 'under', use hand signs to support their understanding of these words. If anyone in your setting is trained in Signalong or Makaton, they will be able to teach you the signs for 'on' and 'under'.
Alternatively, place a fisted hand on top of a flat hand when you say the word 'on'. Whilst holding the flat hand still, place the fisted hand below the flat hand whilst saying the word 'under'.

Activity 10: Bean bag toss

Why? Active games such as the bean bag toss are motivating and fun ways to help children understand and consolidate their vocabulary.

Resources: Three large hoops, a selection of bean bags. Large action picture cards with pictures of people doing different actions such as running, swimming, painting, reading, sleeping, eating and drinking.

How?
Set the three hoops out next to each other in a row, use a marker to show children where to stand.
Place an action picture card in each hoop.
Say the action to the child.
The child aims the bean bag into the hoop with the correct action picture.
Change the action pictures around once everyone has had a turn.

Helpful hint: Change the action pictures around and ask children to name the action and choose the hoop to throw into.

Get active!

Activity 11: Lifeboats

Why? It is a fast-paced, fun game for a large group that enables children to understand and follow a range of movement instructions, and develop their vocabulary, using language linked to boats and ships.

Resources: Choose from spots, hoops, carpet squares, or some type of non-slip markers.

How?
Spread out the markers around the space, one for each child. Explain that the game is set at sea and they are all on a big ship. They are the sailors and have to follow the instructions of the captain (you). They do different movements to each instruction.

INSTRUCTIONS
Lifeboats = all stand on a marker/hoop, these are their lifeboats that are all on the big ship and they can jump into any of them once the game starts
Explain the sides of the room/area are the front, back and sides of the big ship,

Port = left
Starboard = right
Bow = front
Stern = back
Just use 2 to begin with

When you shout out these words they run to the correct side of the room.

Climb the ladder = pretend to climb ladder
Salute the captain = salute
Scrub the decks = pretend to scrub floor
Row ashore = sit in lifeboat and pretend to row
Overboard = fall out of lifeboat into sea
Swim ashore = swim on tummies or backs!
Land ahoy = look through telescope
Shark attack = shout help and get to any lifeboat as quickly as possible.

Helpful hint: Only introduce a few instructions at a time and practise, for example. just directions and lifeboats to start with. When they are familiar with the game, children could take turns to be the captain.

Activity 12: Pizza massage

Why? This is a lovely, relaxing and calming activity. It helps children to understand and use food vocabulary. It helps children to be comfortable with appropriate touch, and to develop their sensitivity.

Resources: A comfortable place, your hands or a soft ball to roll on the backs of the children who are wary of personal contact.

How?
Massage a child's back as they lie on their tummy. Always ask the child for their permission to do a pizza massage.
Knead the dough gently with your fingers.
Spread on the tomato paste with the palms of your hands.
Ask the child what they would like on their pizza, ham, mushrooms, tomatoes, sweetcorn, etc. and pretend to put this all over, with gentle presses.
Sprinkle cheese all over with gentle finger play.
Cut the pizza into slices using the side of your hand in criss-cross motion.

Helpful hint: Children can give you a pizza massage, and also try it on each other. Use a soft ball for a different feel, and if children prefer.

Weather massage:

The sun is shining; make circular movements with flat hands all over the back.
It begins to rain; make raindrops with gentle finger play, faster, then slower as it gradually stops.
The thunder rumbles; massage all over the back.
Lightning strikes; slide the side of the hand across the back in different directions.
It rains again, pitter patter, gentle finger play.
The sun comes out again; make circular movements with flat hands.
A rainbow comes out; make a big arc over the back, sweeping the hands from one side to the other.

Activity 13: Hoop sorting

Why? Being able to sort items into categories is important because it helps children to gain a greater understanding of the meaning of a word.

Resources: Four hoops of different colours, photographs, toy miniatures of real items in each of the following categories:
■ Animals ■ Foods ■ Clothing ■ Toys

How? Start by setting out just two coloured hoops, a metre or two apart.

Explain to the children that you are going to be sorting out all the things in the big pile

Put one or two items, such as toy animals, in one hoop, and put one or two items from a different category, such as toy food, in the other hoop.

Let the children pick items from a pile of different objects

They then have to run to the correct hoop and place the item in the hoop

If the children can manage two categories, make this activity more difficult by adding an extra one or two hoops.

Helpful hint: If children are good at this, see if they can name items in categories without the pictures or items to help them, for example, think of farm animals, thing or places you can visit, think of foods etc.

Activity 14: Hoop play

Why? Children follow instructions to do lots of different activities using their hoops and develop the basic physical skills of jumping, hopping and balancing. Instructions are open-ended, so that children use a playful, problem solving way to interpret the task and respond in their own unique way.

Resources: A hoop for each child and for you, space!

How? Give challenges!
■ jump in and out, 2 feet to 2 feet, 1 foot to the other foot, 1 foot to the same foot (hop)
■ jump in and out sideways, backwards and forwards
■ leap over it – a more challenging jump!
■ put feet inside and walk hands around the outside, and vice versa
■ put bottom inside and 1 foot and 1 hand outside, play around doing this with different body parts
■ give open-ended challenges, such as put 3 bits of your body inside and 1 outside
■ balance on 2 parts of your body inside the hoop
■ pretend it's a puddle and splash in it, jump over it, stamp in it
■ take your whole body through the hoop and jump through it (like a skipping rope)
■ with a partner, one holding the hoop, find different ways of getting through it on hands and feet, back, tummy.

Helpful hint: Ask questions that all children can interpret in their own way, including children with a physical disability.

Get active!

Activity 15: Telling stories through movement

Why? By acting out stories, children will remember them, understand the story better, know about the beginning, middle and end, understand the sequence of the story, the characters and the language. They will recall their knowledge of the story and be able to reflect on, adapt and explore their ideas and own understanding.

Resources: Books with a 'movement' element, see list below.

How? Make sure the children are familiar with the story before they begin to represent it through movement. Know the story well yourself so that you can develop the key movement aspects.

- Practise telling it without the book
- Work out the type of movements that will represent the story best, for example, how the different fish move in the 'Rainbow Fish', how the dinosaurs move, and other animals in 'Doing the Animal Bop'.
- Think how you might best describe these movements, for example, small fish may 'dart', change direction quickly, are light and quick. Lions may 'prowl', moving slowly, smoothly and heavily through the jungle. Snakes 'squirm and wiggle', are slow and fast.

Helpful hint: You can choose to use elements of the story, for example, the animal movements, or follow the whole story, or both.

You can practise and develop some aspects of the story before you go through the main story, for example the fish, giant or animal movements. This may be enough for the first session.

Under 2s
When sharing books, emphasise the sounds and actions in the story; make it physical for the child, for example, use your hands to creep up their legs and arms for Incy Wincy spider, and tickle them, for Hickory Dickory Dock sway them from side to side for 'tick tock', let them fall gently through your legs for Humpty Dumpty, move their legs up and down for the Grand Old Duke of York, hide under some material just like Spot hides.

Telling traditional fairy stories through movement

Resources: Books with a 'movement' element.

How? Make sure the children are familiar with the story, and you can tell it without the book!
Explore the movement elements and the language within the story.
How does Little Red Riding Hood move? She might skip happily through the forest. How do the trees move? They are very tall and move slowly in the breeze. How does the wolf move? Slyly and slowly creeping through the forest.
Ask the children to become the various characters and natural features.
For example, the trees in the wood, the river flowing fast under the bridge, the beanstalk winding up to the sky.

Books for telling movement stories (there are lots more!)

Lost in the Snow, Ian Beck
Small Bear Lost, Martin Wadell
Mr Wolf's Week, Colin Hawkins
Beautiful Bananas, Elizabeth Laird, Liz Pichon
The Dance of the Dinosaurs, Colin and Jacqui Hawkins
Bumpus Jumpus Dinosaurumpus, Tony Mitton and Guy Parker-Rees
Where's the Gold? Pamela Allen
Doing the Animal Bop, Jan Ormerod and Lindsey Gardiner
Follow my Leader, Simon Puttock and Philip Hopman
We're Going on a Bear Hunt, Michael Rosen and Helen Oxenbury
We're Going on a Lion Hunt, David Axell
Walking through the Jungle, Julie Latcome
Rainbow Fish and the Sea Monster's Cave, Marcus Pfister
Whoosh around the Mulberry Bush, Jan Ormerod and Lindsey Gardiner
If You're Happy and you Know it! Jan Ormerod and Lindsey Gardiner
Little Red, Lynn Roberts
Stick Man, Julia Donaldson and Alex Scheffler.

Tables of development

Understanding

Receptive language typical developmental milestones	
Age	**Stage**
By 6 months	Understands words such as 'no', 'bye bye', 'all gone' 'more', when these words are used in context and accompanied with gestures.
7-12 months	Recognises their own name, the names of familiar people and objects, such as 'daddy', 'car', 'teddy', 'trees', 'toast'.
1-2 years	Points to items when you name them, for example, 'where's the cat?' Follows simple requests, for example, 'give me the ball'. Answers simple questions, for example, 'more juice?'
2-3 years	Understands and follows two-part instructions, such as 'put the bricks back in the box please'. Understands certain concepts, such as big/little, high/low.
3-4 years	Follows more lengthy instructions with 3 or more key words, for example, 'put the bricks in the box on the shelf'. Understands and answers simple questions of who, what, and where.

(Based on Bowen, 1998)

Section 4: Active Talking

Why is it important?

○ Speech Sounds

● **Talking**

○ Understanding

○ Social Communication

○ Attention and Listening

'Language acquisition through movement cannot be underestimated' (Maude, 2010)

Statutory Framework for the EYFS (2017) Early Learning Goals

Speaking: children express themselves effectively, showing awareness of listeners' needs. They use past, present and future forms accurately when talking about events that have happened or are to happen in the future. They develop their own narratives and explanations by connecting ideas or events.

This section is all about prompting the spoken, or **expressive** language skills of the children in your setting.

Expressive language is a term that refers to a person's ability to use words to convey meaning to others.

It is about communicating with others through spoken language, and expressing our thoughts for a purpose. In order to successfully use language in a meaningful way, a child needs to have developed a good **understanding** of language.

Talking, or using expressive language, is a complex process, which includes the physical action of forming the words in the mouth. This aspect will be explored in Section 5: Active Speech Sounds. The tricky task of talking is dependent on the competent use of a number of other thinking skills. Think about the following scenario:

Imagine you are talking to a friend about your plans for the weekend. What do you need to do to be able to tell them about your plans?

You must be able to:

■ organise your thoughts (remember what you are going to do and in what order)
■ think about the message you want to get across, *choose the right words (so that others understand)*
■ place words in the correct order (so that it makes sense)
■ use grammar correctly (for example, tenses)
■ construct questions (so, for example, that you can ask your friend what they are doing at the weekend too)

During language development, children understand a lot more than they can say themselves. This is why talking comes after understanding on the Communication Climbing Frame. In order to talk well, a child must be able to understand language well.

Based on developmental milestones, it is expected that, by the time children are 4-5 years of age, they are usually able to speak in lengthy utterances and can describe events, retell stories, and answer questions without too much effort.

They can explain what they want and need as well as share their thoughts and ideas.

Take a look at The Communication Chain on page 5, which highlights the key processes involved in talking. For successful communication to take place, a person must have an idea they want to communicate, choose the words to use and then plan how to combine these words so that they makes sense.

Talking

From the day they are born, children make sounds and noises. Although newborn babies cannot use words, they are still communicating. The noises that babies make differ, depending on whether they are experiencing discomfort, pleasure or finding out what their voice can do. Bowen (1998) highlights that, within their first three months of life, babies use a different cry depending on the message they are communicating, for example, the cry they make when they are hungry is not the same as the cry they make when they are in pain.

Reflection

Consider your key group of children and see whereabouts they are on the developmental milestones on page 76. Remember that there are many variations in 'typical' development.

Section 4: Active Talking: Why is it important?

Statutory Framework for the EYFS (2017)

One of the three characteristics of effective learning is: **creating and thinking critically** - children have and develop their own ideas, make links between ideas, and develop strategies for doing things

By around 6 months, children are typically babbling and experimenting more with their voice. This can be referred to as 'vocal play'. At times, they can indicate that they want something using sounds or gestures. This is all part of language development; babies are experimenting with their voice as well as finding ways to get their messages across to their care givers.

The list below gives examples of ways in which a young child might communicate before they are able to use words.

- Babbling
- Making sounds
- Laughing
- Reaching out
- Looking
- Pointing
- Taking others by the hand to what they want
- Waving
- Crying
- Smiling
- Copying sounds
- Facial expressions
- Body movements (e.g. kicks, wiggles).

There are key developmental milestones that children will go through when learning to talk. Children usually say their first words at around 12 months of age. This of course can vary by a few months and still be considered typical. By around 2 years of age, children start to join words together. By the time a child is about 3 years old, they are joining several (3+) words together.

Remember that all children develop at different rates. Some children start talking early and appear to be advanced compared to other children, and some children start talking slightly later than the average child. All this can be considered to be 'normal' development. There is a general table of typical language development on page 76.

Case study: Ralph, 3 years 2 months
Ralph joins 4+ words together
He uses language for a range of purposes, for example, he greets others, talks about things that interest him, asks questions and makes requests.

Ralph's talking skills are age-appropriate.

Case study: Martina, 3 years   PART 1
Martina uses 1 or 2 words at a time, for example, 'juice', 'daddy gone'.
When she needs help with something she will usually rely on gestures, for example, pulling nursery staff by the hand and then pointing to an item that is out of reach.

She seems to experience some frustration as a result of not being able to express herself fully and parents report that she has regular tantrums at home.

Martina has delayed talking skills.

There is more information about the steps that staff have taken to support Martina with her talking skills.
See Case study: Martina PART 2 page 71.

When looking at language development, it is helpful to categorise words into different groups so that you can identify the progress children make, and focus on specific types of vocabulary.

- Naming words (nouns/objects) – teddy, car, tummy
- People names – mummy, daddy,
- Social words – hello, bye, please
- Action words (verbs) – jump, sing, run
- Location words (prepositions) – in, down, up
- Describing words (adjectives) – soft, little, big.

Children are likely to use the naming words for the things and the people that they are most familiar with, for example, a favourite toy or food, before being able to use action words, location words and describing words. (Lindon, 2012)

The more often a child hears a word and phrase in a meaningful situation, the more likely they are to start using the words and phrases themselves (*Principle 1:* Children need to hear many words often). Research suggests that children need to hear a word multiple times before they can use the word appropriately themselves. '*Young children need plenty of relaxed opportunities to hear words in their relevant contexts before they are likely to say the word spontaneously*'. (Harries, 2013)

Sustained Shared Thinking

'*Sustained shared thinking' occurs when two or more individuals 'work together' in an intellectual way to solve a problem, clarify a concept, evaluate an activity, extend a narrative etc. Both parties must contribute to the thinking and it must develop and extend the understanding.*'
The Effective Provision of Pre-School Education (EPPE) Project (2004).

Talking comes from the thoughts we have. We speak our thoughts, although as adults we learn not to speak all of them! We often speak as we are thinking, 'we think out loud' as it were. Young children think out loud most of the time, often saying what comes into their mind. This action of 'thinking out loud' develops their understanding of language while enabling them to continue a conversation along a train of thought. Attention and listening skills are being used at their highest level, and this is essential for learning of this depth to take place.

Sustained Shared Thinking happens when adults and children, or children talking and playing together are totally engrossed with each other either in a conversation or an activity. Everyone is on the same wavelength and feels so connected that they are intent on pursuing the task in hand. This can happen anytime and anywhere and is about 'the meeting of minds' and the learning that takes place for everyone involved.

The EPPE Project (2004) found that the most effective settings encouraged sustained shared thinking.

Here is an example given by Iram Siraj-Blatchford and Laura Manni (Nursery World, 2004)

Grace (aged four): 'How did God make us?'
Adult: 'I don't know. What do you think?'
Grace: 'I don't know.'
Adult: 'Well, how would you make yourself?'
Grace: 'I would make myself happy.'
Tom (aged four): 'I think when God made us, we made God.'
Grace: 'He putted (sic) our bones in first, and then he putted blood on the bones, and then he putted our skin on.'
Tom: 'No - he opened up our bones and put the blood in us.'
Grace: 'No - if he put it in our bones, the blood wouldn't come out.'

Open questions, such as 'what do you think?' 'How does that work, do you think?' prompt speculation and an opportunity for children to formulate and express ideas that are still materialising in their mind.

The adult role

'Developing a child's language will support them in developing their other important areas of learning and give them valuable life skills'. (Nash, Lowe, Leah, 2013)

1. Take an active approach

Talk with children about what they are doing and seeing. We naturally talk with young children about what they are doing or seeing at the time.

This is because it is what makes sense to them, for example, the door opens and you say 'here's mummy!' or you point to things and name them, such as an aeroplane, a tractor or a ball. We comment on their actions, such as 'Wow! You are running fast!' or 'You are feeding your teddy'.

We ask questions about 'doing' things, such as 'Shall we go to the park?' or 'Shall we put your shoes on?' The language we use with children is usually about their actions, or the actions they make the toys do, such as 'Choo choo! The train is going through the tunnel'.

Give children words for what their bodies do. This means noticing and commenting on their movements. Young children do many random movements like twirling, spinning on their bottom, or lying upside down with their legs against the furniture or wall. We are inclined to ignore this activity, tending not to value it as much as other things they do. These movements are important to them, because they are the movements their bodies are seeking in order to develop and grow. (Jabadao, 2007)

The vocabulary for their own movements can be rich and meaningful to them and so be memorable. So, if you say for example, 'You are lying upside down with your legs against the wall', there are many different types of words to understand, which they can absorb and use themselves in time.

As children make up rules for active games like hide and seek and chase, they naturally negotiate, argue, laugh and chat, communicating socially at high levels to cooperate and make things work.

2. Play and Interact

As a key person, you play a fundamental role in helping babies and young children to communicate and talk. Through everyday conversations, you nurture their confidence in speaking as they tell you about their experiences at home. You are the person with whom they feel most at ease and therefore are the most likely person who will listen to them and appreciate their attempts to express themselves. Your sensitive interaction will help them use new words and express their thoughts and feelings.

'A flow of conversation that is responsive to a child's interests and abilities is essential to their language and wider development'. (Nash, Lowe and Leah, 2013)

- **Have conversations with children, from birth!** Talking is a social activity that involves taking turns to speak and listen. (**See Section 2: Social Communication**). As adults and practitioners, it is easy to fall into the habit of telling children to do things, giving them instructions, telling them about things, and not spending time **listening** to them and waiting for them to formulate their thoughts. When talking to babies, pause and wait for them to gurgle back, they soon understand the turn taking, the basis for their future language interactions.

- **Talk to children at the right level**. It usually comes naturally to match your language level to the child's. For example with babies we use simple expressive language with exaggerated facial expressions. For 2-3 year olds we have 'proper' conversations with longer and more complex sentences. See page 68 for help with speaking at the right level to children for their age and stage of development.

- **Develop Sustained Shared Thinking** with children. Tune in to children's interests and fascinations so that you can develop prolonged and deep conversations with them. Recognise times when you can help children to work things out by asking open questions and commenting helpfully when children are persevering with a task. Try some of the following ways to extend children's thinking and ability to express their thoughts.

  - How did that happen, I wonder?
  - How could you find out?
  - What do you think?
  - Do you think everyone else would think the same?
  - What do you think is happening?
  - I don't know, what do you think?
  - Can you tell me more about that?
  - How can you make/build this?
  Siraj-Blatchford, Laura Manni (2004)

- **Get down to the child's level**, to have direct eye contact during a conversation; this shows a genuine interest in what they have to say, and shows that you are listening intently and have time for them.

- **Copy the noises and sounds** that the babies and toddlers make even if they are just noises rather than words. This shows that you are responsive to a child's interests and abilities and will encourage them to experiment further with their voice.
  (*Principle 3:* Children learn best when adults are responsive to them)

- **Have fun together with your voices**. Singing familiar sounds, making silly noises and making animal and vehicle noises helps children enjoy, practise and gain confidence in using their voice. (Signalong, 2010)

- **Comment on what the child is doing and is interested in**. If you are outside for example, and a child points at a bird, simply name it for them, 'bird...that's a bird, tweet tweet!' If the child is building with blocks, you could say things like 'you're building, 1, 2, 3', 'red brick, blue brick'.

- **Add to what the child says**. For example, if a child says 'dog', you could say 'yes, a big dog!'

- **Give the child time to communicate**. For example, if a child drops his toast, many adults would automatically pick it up straight away. In situations like this, try giving the child time to try and communicate a message to you.

- **Use language that is slightly ahead** of the language that they child is using. For example, if you're playing with a child who is using 1-2 words for example, 'car', 'car fast', use 3-5 words phrases, for example, 'wow, a fast car!, ready, steady, go!' 'that's a bus'. This way, children will start to see how they can extend their language. You are essentially modelling the next step for children.

- **Rephrase what the child says** so that it is grammatically correct. Do this in a natural way that is part of the conversation and enables children to absorb new ways to say things. For example, if a child says 'Look, mouses!', you could say 'Oh yes, mice!', 'Wow, they're tiny mice!'
(Primary National Strategy, 2007)
(*Principle 5:* Vocabulary and grammar are learned together)

- **Build strong bonds and relationships with your key group**, so that children want to talk to you and are confident to have a go without being afraid of making mistakes. Generally, children naturally become quieter with people they don't know so well.

- **Ask parents for the special words** their child uses for family members, everyday events and objects in their lives.

- **Be responsive** with a smile, an expressive face and enthusiasm to all attempts a child makes to talk.

- **Read with children**. Research shows that reading with children supports their language development. *'Book reading consistently has been found to have the power to create interactional contexts that nourish language development'*. Books motivate children to communicate and, when parents respond to what the child is interested in, it helps the child to learn to new words. (Dickinson et al, 2012)

- **Identify the important language children can learn in different play areas**. Children learn different vocabulary and ideas as they play with different materials and in a range of play areas. It is useful to identify specific words and phrases for the different play areas in your nursery, and for the activities you plan. Even though this comes naturally as you play alongside children, it helps to think about these beforehand so that you can interact effectively to increase children's vocabulary and understanding.

  - **In role play scenarios**, they first of all play out family scenarios and try out the mummy and daddy language, such as 'I'm going to work', 'I'm feeding the baby' or 'I'm taking the dog for a walk', and sometimes things we don't expect to hear that they have picked up from home!
  - **In sensory play** they describe what things feel like and look like, such as 'squishy', 'silky', 'crinkled'
  - **In physical play** there is a wide range of positional language such as up and down, behind, inside, over, higher etc. and action verbs like jumping, running, kicking, climbing, and body parts, such as reach with your hands, bend your knees, put your tummy on there.

3. Create the best environment

- **Create 'Communication friendly spaces'** (Elks and McLachlan, 2016)
A communication-friendly space makes communication as easy, effective and enjoyable as possible. A communication friendly environment supports the development of all children's communication skills, including those with speech and language difficulties and learning EAL. There are lots of inspiring ways of creating special places for talking, both permanent and temporary. These can range from a 'boat' outdoors, a willow structure, a hollow barrel or a large pipe, tents and dens or a large box. Think about small places for one child to talk to themselves and imagine in private, or for two to chat, and also spaces for a small group of children to play together.

- **Move through different environments throughout the day** with your babies, toddlers and young children both inside and outside, so that they are motivated to talk about different things, places and the natural world and that you have different things, places, and 'happenings' to talk about and point out to your children.

- **Provide a good range of interesting resources and experiences**, so that children are motivated to express themselves in different contexts. Children need to experience things before they can talk about them. Different play situations lend themselves to different vocabulary.

- **Provide multi-sensory experiences**. Physical and sensory experiences make words meaningful to children. The language children use is based on what they are hearing, feeling, smelling and touching. For example children will use the word 'slimy' when they play with slime (soap flakes and water mix), and squidgy if they are playing with dough. Not all children have access to a range of multi-sensory experiences when at home so it is vital that they get these experiences within your setting.

- **Provide voice changers** such as microphones, karaoke machines, recording devices to encourage children to explore how their own voice can magically change!

- **Provide talking equipment**, such as telephones, Walkie Talkies, loud speakers, karaoke machines, and voice recording equipment to encourage children to use their voices, explore what they can do and for purposeful communication.

- **Provide a stage area, or 'story chair' indoors and outdoors** to encourage performance and telling stories aloud to others. Make sure you have a wide range of dressing-up clothes that encourage children to try out being different characters, and using words and phrases that a policeman, doctor or waiter may use.

- **Provide a range of role-play scenarios** that warrant different **situation-based** language, such as a shop, a doctor's surgery, a garage, a builder's yard, a café.

- **Reduce background noise**. As highlighted in all of the previous sections, limiting background noise makes it easier for children to listen, assimilate information and to speak, without distraction and, for example, without the numbing monotony of constant nursery rhymes. As we all know, trying to converse against music in a noisy bar is hard work!

4. Work with parents

We know that it is through hearing models of communication that babies and toddlers start to understand and then use words themselves. Some children may not be spoken to or listened to at home by the adults in the household. This is unfortunately very common, particularly with the increase in smart phones, tablets etc. Be aware that some parents don't recognise the importance of talking to babies from birth.

Emphasise the importance of their role in talking to their children at home to develop their speaking skills.

Share the progress their child is making with talking, with certain activities at nursery.

Suggest they continue successful activities at home that are working well in the nursery.

Model strategies from the **Adult Role: Play and Interact** section, when parents are around. For example, copy the sounds that their baby is making or comment on what their toddler is doing.

Use your newsletter or web page for articles about good practice. For example, 'How to help your toddler talk!' or post relevant research articles.

Encourage the sharing of information between home and your setting. Ask what new words they have said at home, tell parents what they have said in the setting. Find out where they went at the weekend so you can talk about it, and explain the kinds of activities that you have been doing in your setting.

5. Support children who are learning EAL

This section has highlighted that children's understanding is ahead of their talking. This also applies to second language learning. Children learning EAL will be absorbing and understanding English before they start to speak it.

Children who are learning EAL may already have language skills in their first language. A child's abilities in their home language(s) will vary from child to child; some will have age-appropriate home language skills and others will have advanced or delayed skills, just like children whose first language is English.

Learning an additional language is different to learning a first language. Most EAL children will have a certain level of knowledge about language. They will understand that words refer to objects and events, words can be combined to form phrases and sentences, and that by applying grammatical rules tenses can be changed (Madhani in Buckley, 2003). This knowledge gives children a range of strategies to apply when learning an additional language.

The rate at which a child learning EAL picks up and begins to use English depends on a number of factors, including their level of self-esteem and confidence. Many children learning EAL go through a 'silent phase', sometimes for an extended period of time (Primary National Strategy, 2007). The child will be listening and learning, but not necessarily speaking, perhaps for a couple of weeks or even up to six months. (Watkinson, 2009)

For children who are going through a 'silent' period, it is vital that adults are patient and continue to play and interact with the child in ways that will help develop their understanding of English. Refer back to, **Section 3: Active Understanding, Adult Role**.

It is important to be aware that some children will not attempt to answer questions unless they know that their answer is definitely correct. In some cultures *'an incorrect answer or a guess may mean losing face or being humiliated.'* (Mistry and Sood, 2015)

Pre-school children who are learning EAL will still be learning their home language(s). These children need to have sufficient exposure to both languages to develop good skills in both languages. It is therefore important to ensure that parents understand the importance of continuing to speak their home language with their child(ren) at home.

> *'Practitioners have a key role in reassuring parents that maintaining and developing their home language will benefit their children and support their developing skills in English.'*
> (Primary National Strategy, 2007)

Case study: Amiir, 3 years 6 months
First language: Somali

Amiir is the oldest child in his family. He has one younger brother. At home everyone in the family speaks Somali and they have done since he was born. When Amiir started nursery at the age of 3 years and 2 months he didn't know any English.

During the first couple of weeks, Amiir was very quiet at nursery. He would play near other children but would back away when other children spoke to him.

His key person, Natasha, noticed that Amiir got more and more involved with the other children and started attempting English words, starting with naming words (nouns).

His mum doesn't speak any English. Fortunately one of the staff who works in a different room, speaks Somali, which meant that she was able to develop a good relationship with Amiir's mother and alongside Natasha, fill her in about Amiir's day when she picked him up.

Amiir now loves being at nursery and gets involved in all sorts of activities and games every day. He is now putting words together in English and is attempting new words daily.

6. Provide extra support for children with difficulties

Remember that all children develop at different rates. Children vary greatly in the way their speech skills develop. However, in your setting, you might notice that there are a few children who aren't able to talk as much or as well as other children of their age. This could be for a number of different reasons.

Difficulties with areas further down the Communication Climbing Frame

If a child is struggling with talking, it is likely that they have difficulties with some of the areas further down the Communication Climbing Frame, perhaps understanding, or listening. Talking skills are dependent on competence in these vital underpinning skills. Identify the stage at which the child is struggling and give them suitable support. Follow the advice and strategies highlighted in the previous sections.

Delayed language skills

The figures in the introduction highlight that more and more children are reaching school age with delayed language skills. Children with delayed language skills are learning the same skills that all children learn, however they are behind in reaching their developmental milestones. For example, a child who is 3 years who is only just starting to join two words together may simply have delayed expressive language skills. To support children with delayed talking skills, daily good practice with lots of adult interaction is key.

Talk on a one to one and have small groups. The key to learning to talk is to talk! Spending time getting to know the child, listening, building confidence and having conversations is essential to all children's language development. Carry out some of the activities suggested in this section and previous sections every day.

Comment, comment, comment! When supporting children who have talking difficulties, make more comments and ask fewer questions!

More specific difficulties with learning language skill
Other children, despite good development in other areas, may struggle with spoken language. Many of these children struggle to pick up the rules of language. They may have strengths in some language areas and difficulties in others. For example they may have a very good vocabulary and know many long and sophisticated words however they may struggle to put words in the correct order.

Model good language. If you notice that there are particular parts of talking that the child finds difficult, model these during a range of different activities. For example, if you notice that the child only uses naming words, model verbs when they are playing in the sand as well as when they are eating a snack! Comment on what is happening around the child, and reword what the child says in a positive way.

Use a signing support system such as Signalong or Makaton when communicating with children with language difficulties. Signs are simply hand gestures that are used to accompany the words that you say. This supports children to understand what you're saying and gives them an alternative way in which to communicate when they don't have the words for what they want to say.

Other children may have problems developing their talking skills due to other difficulties, such as learning disabilities or autism spectrum condition. (See page 37 for advice about supporting children who have autism).

Reluctant talkers / Selective mutism
Some children have developed expressive language skills, and are able to talk and use these skills in some settings but not in others. It is important to be aware that these children are not making a choice not to talk, they are unable to talk in some situations, due to anxiety. (Johnson, 2001). So even though 'selective mutism' implies that it is the child's choice, this is most often not the case.

> 'Selective Mutism is thought to reflect a fear of being heard (or seen) speaking in some situations, leading a child to speak in some settings while not in others.' (McHolm, Cunningham and Vanier, 2005)

If you have a child who is not talking in your setting, but who is able to talk in other settings it is important to create a relaxed, welcoming and friendly atmosphere, where the child can feel secure, comfortable and peaceful. Within this environment, it is vital that they develop a strong relationship with the key person, who can nurture their interests, communicate in a range of ways, and help them join in play with others. The child is more likely to have the confidence to talk when they have developed a trusting relationship with their key person.

It is important to be patient, accept them for how they are and not put pressure on them to talk. Accept easily the child's non-verbal responses, for example, let them point to the fruit that they would like at snack time rather than using words. If and when the child does speak, it is important to simply respond to what they have said, rather than acting surprised and drawing too much attention to the fact that they have spoken.

Case study: Martina, 3 years   **PART 2**
Martina was introduced earlier in this chapter (page 64)

She will often rely on gestures and other norms of non-verbal communication (such as pointing) to communicate with others. Sometimes however she will use single words or two words together.

When she started at nursery, all of the staff were concerned about her limited ability to use words. Mum has also expressed her concern since Martina started nursery.

Mum expressed her concern about Martina's language when she began nursery.

Nursery staff have included Martina in a small language group for 15 minutes every day. They use a range of multi-sensory activities and Martina has recently started to use the words 'up' and 'down' during bubble activities.

Reflection

Compare the following examples:

Adult 1: 'What's that?' 'What have you got?', 'What are you doing?', 'Where does it go?'
Adult 2: 'Wow, you're building'. 'Big tower', '1, 2, 3', 'It's a blue brick', 'Ooh crash!'

Adult 1 asks multiple questions and a child with language difficulties is unlikely to be able to answer these.
Adult 2 models words and phrases for the child, rather than putting demands on the child.

Get active!

Activity 1: What's in the bag?

Why? Hiding items in a bag adds a sense of excitement to a simple activity and encourages children to say the name of the object.

Resources: A small draw-string bag and a selection of toys, for example:

- Toy animal figures and a farm or a zoo scene
- Doll's house furniture and doll's house
- Teddy or doll and clothing to fit the teddy or doll
- vehicles and a track or car mat.

How? Start with a selection of toy items from one category (e.g. toy animals). Make sure that these are not in the view of the children
Place one toy item in the bag (without the children seeing)
Tell the children that you are all going to sing 'the feely bag' song.
'What's in the bag?'
'What's in the bag?'
'[Child's name]' have a look and see what's inside!'
Use an adult to model first if possible.

If modelling with an adult, after you sing the song, say 'It's Miss X's turn...' and hand the bag to the adult.
The adult should open the bag and pull out the toy item.
The adult should simply name the item 'It's a dog!'

Each time an item is pulled out of the bag, encourage all children to join in actively, for example, encourage all children to make the noise of a dog, make a train noise and a long train of children.

Then the person whose turn it was then gets to place the toy wherever they like in the scene and comment on what they have done, for example, 'The dog is on the grass', 'The horse is in the pond'.

Helpful hint: When using the teddy/doll and the clothing, place the items of clothing in the bag for the children to pick out and name. Then see if the children can tell you where on the body the clothes go.

Activity 2: Book buddies

Why? Research shows that reading with children supports their language development.

Resources: Books, books and more books! Picture books, noisy books, feely books, pop-up books! Any books that capture the interest of the children!

How? Follow the child's lead when looking at books together
Don't worry about trying to read every word from start to finish
Name things and talk about what you can see with your child
'When you read a book with your child, abandon your agenda. Let your child lead, and talk about whatever interests him or her'. (Hanen Website)

Helpful hint: You can encourage a child to participate by simply pausing. Story sacks can be an exciting addition to the experience of looking at a book. Simply gather together items from a story and pull them out of the bag when reading the book!

Activity 3: Fruit tasting

Why? Fruit comes in a variety of colours, sizes, shapes, textures and flavours; therefore it is perfect for tasting and talking about. Children can talk about the fruit, what it looks like, smells like, tastes like, and whether they like it or not.

Resources: A selection of fruits, for example, bananas, apples, pears, oranges, peach, plum, grapes, strawberries, kiwis and plates.

Peel or prepare the fruits beforehand but ensure that one of each fruit is left whole so that the children can relate the cut-up pieces to the whole fruit.

How? Explain to the children that you are going to be tasting some yummy fruits together. Make sure all children have washed their hands.

- Select a fruit from the range available
- Start with one of the more commonly eaten fruits like an apple, banana or orange
- Look at the whole fruit together
- Encourage the children to name the fruit and then talk about the colour, size, shape and texture
- Talk about the colour, size, shape and texture of the fruit
- Ask open questions such as, 'what does it feel like? Smell like?
- Then encourage the children to taste the fruit and say if they like it or not
- After you have tried several fruits together, ask the children which fruit is their favourite.

Helpful hint: For fussy eaters, start with a fruit that you know they like. When offering new fruits, cut them up into very small pieces to make it less daunting. Encourage them to simply lick the food if they are reluctant to eat it. This way they can still make a comment about the taste/texture/flavour of the food. ALWAYS CHECK FOR ALLERGIES!

Activity 4: Touchy feely boxes

Why? Feely boxes encourage children to start using describing words, such as 'big', 'little', 'soft', 'bumpy', 'slimy', 'hard'.

Resources: Several feely boxes. These can be bought or they can be easily made. To make a feely box, simply cut a hole in a cardboard box big enough for hands to fit inside. Then snip the toes off an old sock and attach it to the hole in the box so that the children can't see what is inside but can feel what's there.

A selection of items that are different in texture:
- Something soft like a feather, a soft toy, or cotton wool
- Something hard like a stone, a shell or a building brick
- Something slimy like a peeled grape
- Something bumpy like a Lego brick
- Something squishy like a sponge
- Something rough like sandpaper
- Something spikey like a hairbrush

Put one thing inside each box.

How? Explain to the children that they are going to be feeling lots of different things in the boxes, and that the things have to stay inside the box until they've finished the game.

Feel some items together as a group (without using the feely boxes). Start by feeling a soft toy, then feel an item such as a toothbrush.

Talk with the children about how the items feel, using words like 'spikey', 'soft', 'slimy' etc.

Then encourage the children to put their hands in the feely boxes and describe what the item feels like.

If they're struggling to find the words that they need, give them options, ask them 'is it hard or soft?'

Model this for the children too, put your hand in a feely box and describe how the item feels 'ooh, it feels soft'

Can they guess what it is? Then take it out of the box.

Helpful hint: If a child pulls the item out of the feely box straight away, don't worry. Simply support the child to feel the item more and talk together about how it feels.

Get active!

Activity 5: Bug hunt

Why? Children will be motivated to talk about what they have found so they can share their excitement with you and others.

Resources: An outdoor space, ideally somewhere with long grass, trees and shrubs. If you have a wildlife garden on site, that is absolutely perfect for a bug hunt.
Magnifying glasses for children (one per child in the group)
Clear plastic containers with small holes in the lids.
A plastic spoon or spades for each child (to be used for picking up bugs!)
Optional: A selection of plastic insects, Tablet, an interactive whiteboard, books and posters about bugs.

How? Show children some video clips of a range of insects, or look at books, posters and plastic insects and talk about them
Go outside to look for bugs together
Demonstrate how to use the magnifying glass and explain about being gentle and careful when collecting the bugs
Then take the children outside and let them go off (within a restricted area) to hunt for bugs
Staff should help children, suggesting they look under stones, wood and dig in the soil etc.
When a child finds an insect, they will more often than not come and tell an adult
Use this as the perfect opportunity to spark a conversation with the child about what they have found. Chat about

colours, number of legs, wings, how it moves, what they think it eats, where did they find it and listen carefully to the child's ideas about the insect, where it lives and if they have a family and what they think it does. They are likely to have some vivid imaginative ideas!

**Helpful hint: Gather children together in small groups to share and talk about each other's finds. Use group or circle time to chat about their discoveries.
Sing 'Incy Wincy spider' and 'There's a worm at the bottom of the garden'.
Read stories connected to bugs, like 'Billy's Beetle' by Mick Inkpen and 'The Very Quiet Cricket' by Eric Carle.**

Activity 6: Messy and tactile play recipes (there are so many of these available on various websites, but here are a few easy ones)

Why? Messy and tactile play provokes talking and new vocabulary about what the substance feels like, smells like, and what it does. It sparks scientific thinking when it is made, about how the substance behaves and what happens when it is mixed with other stuff. It triggers the imagination too.

How? Most of these can be made with the children
Play dough that lasts
2 cups of flour (any)
2 cups of water
1 cup of salt
1 tablespoon of oil
1 teaspoon of cream of tartar
Food colouring or paint
Mix altogether, then cook on a low heat stirring continuously until it makes a stretchy lump, leave to cool and knead.
Goop
Add water to cornflour gradually until it becomes silky. It will crumble in your hand if squeezed and drip from a spoon.

Moon dust (Flour sand)
Mix 8 cups of plain flour with 1 cup of vegetable oil, or baby oil. Or just keep adding oil until it feels 'mouldable'! Add colour or glitter for a different experience. Use spoons, moulds, small plant pots, ice cube trays etc.
Can be stored in an airtight container for a few months!
Slime
Mix 1 cup of Soap flakes with 3 cups of warm water and leave overnight. Mix in large bucket.
Coloured rice
Mix 1 cup of rice, 1 tbsp vinegar and food colouring in a zipped plastic bag until all the rice has absorbed the colour. Tip onto a greaseproof lined baking tray and leave to dry for at least four hours.

Activity 7: Finding treasure

Why? This gives children an opportunity to give instructions to others to find hidden 'treasure' and be precise in their language.

Resources: Things to use for treasure, such as old coins, jewellery, small gold and silver items.
Optional: small bags or boxes to put the treasure inside.

How? Children work in 2s or 3s, or a small group with an adult.
Explain to the children that they are going to hide some treasure for their friends to find.
One child hides the treasure in the garden, while the others wait, (could count to 20).
Explain to the child that they need to give the others a 'clue', such as 'near to the climbing frame, inside the playhouse or under a bush.
The other children look for the 'treasure', if they struggle to find it the child gives them another clue.
Take turns to hide and find the treasure.

Helpful hint: With younger children, you give the 'clue' and keep asking them 'what is the clue? As they are looking, and 'where did you find it?' when they return.

Share a story about finding treasure, such as 'Zoe and Beans Pirate Treasure!' by Chloe and Mick Inkpen, or, 'The Treasure of Pirate Frank' by Jez Tuya, or make one up!

Activity 8: Simon says

Why? This gives children an opportunity to give instructions to others and make up their own ideas.

Resources: a small group of children and you the adult!

How? Demonstrate the game of 'Simon says' with the group, giving instructions such as: Simon says...touch your toes,
Simon says...turn around
Simon says...stand on one leg
Run to the fence and back!
Explain that they only do it if 'Simon says', not if you just say the action
Invite each child to take a turn at being 'Simon' and telling the children what to do.

Helpful hint: You can whisper ideas to the child if they struggle, but give them time to think of their own ideas. They will soon get the hang of it and also copy each other's ideas.

Tables of development

Talking

Age	Expressive language developmental stages	Adult interaction
0-12 months	Babies begin with non-verbal expressions and gestures and noises to communicate their needs. By 6 months children start to explore sounds even more. They will use a wider variety of sounds when babbling and copy sounds. Children usually say their first words (not very clearly) at around 12 months old. First words will often be: 'mama', 'dada', 'bye', 'no'.	Interact face to face and use repetitive language with exaggerated facial expressions. Interpret the child's sounds, babbles and expressions and respond so that they learn the cause and effect rules of communication. We are usually very melodic! From 6 months play lots of repetitive interactive games like 'peek a boo'. As they get towards 10 months old, use repetitive language and keep sentences short, emphasizing one main word. Simple repetitive language helps them understand words.
1-2 years	Children start to use more words as each month passes. By 2 years, children will usually be joining 2 words together, for example, 'all gone', 'more ball', 'daddy go', 'no mummy'. They may be asking 2-word questions/ requests by this age too, for example, 'more juice'. From 18 months the language dramatically increases.	Adult follows the child's lead and repeats back the child's words and also adds new language in a melodic way. From 18 months, emphasise certain words in the sentence, and use longer sentences. It is important to make plenty of comments on what the child is doing, using an increasing range of vocabulary for them to understand.
2-3 years	Children quickly develop a wide range of vocabulary. They tend to speak in utterances of 1-3 words or more and can usually make themselves understood to familiar people most of the time. They absorb and copy phrases and explore using new words such as 'actually' and adjectives like, 'huge'. They start to use words from songs and rhymes in real conversations.	Hold short conversations with children about the 'here and now'. Use a wider vocabulary to stimulate the child's growth of language, using descriptive words and words relating to a range of topics.
3-4 years	Children use even longer sentences, for example, combining 4+ words. They start to talk about things that have happened to them, not just talking about the 'here and now'. They are usually keen to talk about a range of topics by this age.	Hold conversations about the 'here and now', things that have happened in the past. Encourage them to re-tell familiar stories. Talk about what things feel like and smell like to develop descriptive words.
4-5 years	Children will typically speak fluently and use relatively long and detailed sentences. They will be using language to reason and ask questions. Children of this age will still make some grammatical mistakes, such as 'I builded it', which does actually follow the grammatical rule of adding 'ed' to something in the past tense, but they haven't learned the exceptions!	Adult interacts to 'fine tune' language and develop it further. Repeat phrases to model correct grammar. Use language as a teaching tool and talking about the world. Ask questions but still comment more and continue with conversations.

(Based on Bowen, 1998)

Remember, at every stage in the table above, children usually understand a lot more than they can say.

Section 5: Active Speech Sounds

Why is it important?

● **Speech Sounds**

○ Talking

○ Understanding

○ Social Communication

○ Attention and Listening

'Children learn sounds by listening to people speaking around them. They have been tuning into the sounds around them since before they were born and they carry on developing their ability to tune into environmental sounds and speech sounds'.
(I CAN, 2016)

This section focuses on the development of speech sounds. 'Speech sounds' come at the very top of the **Communication Climbing Frame** because children need to be able to use a range of words before they can master pronunciation.

Take a look at the **Communication Chain** on page 5, which shows that, in order to talk effectively, we have to physically produce speech in a way that others can understand what we are saying. This involves selecting and articulating speech sounds as well as knowing what to say, choosing the right words and putting them into the right order. It's a tough process!

Babies begin experimenting with sounds not long after birth. They will typically start by making sounds such as 'p', 'b' and 'm' when experimenting with sounds. They will say these with vowel sounds as they babble, such as 'baba', 'mama'.

Reflection

Making sounds with your mouth.

Have a go at saying the sound 'p' out loud.

Think about which parts of the mouth you use to make this sound.
Think about what your mouth actually does when you make this sound.

To make the 'p' sound, you are putting your top and bottom lips together and then releasing to push a burst of air through your lips.

Now make the 'k' sound out loud.

Which parts of the mouth did you use to make this sound?
What did you actually do to produce the sound?

The 'k' sound is made by using the back of the tongue to block off and then quickly release the built up air pressure.

Both of these sounds are made by blocking the air briefly and then releasing the air to say the sound. The 'p' sound is made in this way at the front of the mouth using the lips, whereas the 'k' sound is made at the back of the mouth in the throat.

Now say the 's' sound out loud.

Which parts of the mouth did you use to make this sound?
What did you actually do to produce the sound?

To make the 's' sound, you are creating a vibrating airflow through your front teeth.

Now say the 'f' sound out loud.

What is different about the way we make the 's' sound and the way we make the 'f' sound?

To make the 'f' sound the airflow is restricted by making contact between our top teeth and our lower lip, to make the 's' sound the airflow is restricted by lifting the tongue towards the top of the mouth.

Babies begin by playing with sounds first of all, then babble. This babble develops into longer strings using a wider range of sounds. *(ican.org.uk)*

The previous section explained that children typically say their first words around the 12-month stage. When children start to say words, they will be able to say some sounds in those words. However, they will not yet be able to pronounce all the sounds in the words that they say. Their child-like speech is sometimes difficult to figure out, because they do not yet have the ability to pronounce all of the sounds used in the English language. The development of speech sounds takes place gradually throughout the early years.

Anyone who has tried to communicate in a different language, will know that the pronunciation is usually the least of our worries! We just want to get the words across to be understood. Unfortunately, the pronunciation does sometimes prevent others who are fluent in the language from understanding us! We can, therefore, sympathise greatly with the 2 year old who believes she is saying the words correctly but cannot be understood.

By the time a child is 5 years of age, it is expected that they can be understood by familiar and unfamiliar people almost all of the time. Typical 5 year olds may still have difficulties pronouncing some sounds, for example, 'frog' may be pronounced as 'fwog'. However this does not prevent them from being understood.

There are many different types of sounds. Sounds are made using different parts of the mouth and in different ways. Some sounds are easier to master than others.

So, since sounds are made in different places in the mouth and in different ways, it is no wonder children find it difficult to pronounce some words!

To provide some insight into the complexity of making speech sounds, let's look at the **four different components of speech sounds**, where in the mouth the sound is made, how they are made (what the mouth has to do), vibration sounds, and nasal sounds. This may help you understand children's speech difficulties more specifically and provide more precise help.

Where in the mouth is the sound made? (Place of articulation)

- Some sounds are made at the front of the mouth (p, d. t)
- Some sounds are made at the back of the mouth (k, g)

Different parts of the mouth (vocal organs) are used to create different sounds, the lips, teeth, tongue etc.

How are sounds made? (Manner of articulation)

- Some sounds are made by creating a sustained airflow (f, s, v, z). These can be described as long sounds.

'There is a closing movement of one of the vocal organs, forming such a narrow constriction that it is possible to hear the sound of the air passing through' (Crystal, 2003)

- Some sounds are made by creating a build-up of air and then releasing that build-up (p, t, k). These can be described as short sounds.

'The closing movement is complete, giving a total blockage. The closing movement may involve the lips, the tongue or the throat.' (Crystal, 2003)

Vibration sounds (vocal cord vibrations)

- Some sounds require vibrations of the vocal cords (d, b, m, z). These can be referred to as loud sounds.

- Other sounds require no vibration of the vocal folds (t, p, s). These sounds can be called quiet sounds.

If you touch your throat with a couple of fingers and say the quiet sound 'f' and then the louder sound 'v' you should be able to feel the vibration of your vocal cords when you say the 'v' but not the 'f' sound.

Nasals

The soft palate is the part of the roof of the mouth that is right at the back. Can you feel it with your tongue?

- To make some sounds (including 'm' and 'n'), we have to lower this soft flexible part at the back of the roof of the mouth to allow air to also flow through the nose.

It is now easy to see how complex the process of learning new sounds actually is. This is why development of speech sounds is gradual. Children need to experiment and have a go at using different parts of their mouths in different ways.

In the early years, children are constantly learning new words. When they learn a new word, they have to try and pronounce it. In many cases, they have to attempt a range of movements that their mouths have never tried to make before. It is a bit like learning a complicated dance routine, at first it is very tricky, but you get the hang of it after a while!

The development of speech sounds

'As children are learning to talk, their sound system develops gradually. This means that they cannot say all their sounds straight away, as some are later to develop than others.' (ican.org.uk)

Babies tune into the voices of their parents or carers. They gradually learn to say sounds by listening to others and experimenting with their mouths. Over time they gain greater control over their mouth muscles, making it easier to say the more difficult sounds.

As speech is a complex process to master, children will often swap sounds. They will often swap tricky sounds to say for easier sounds to say. This is a completely typical process that young children go through when their speech is developing.

'Children's speech does not sound like adult speech because they make typical, systematic child-like 'sound replacements' (Bowen,1998)

A common example of a sound replacement: children often swap the sound 'ch' with the easier sound 't', for example, 'cheese' is often pronounced as 'teese'. This is common even at ages 4 and 5.

Words that contain two or more consonants together (e.g. **fl**ower, **st**ring) can be very difficult for young children to pronounce. When learning to say different combinations of sounds, children will often swap sounds or miss off sounds to make words easier to say (e.g. frog often becomes fog or fwog). Again you are likely to still see this in a number of children who are reaching the end of the EYFS.

It is useful to be aware of the stages children go through when developing their skills of pronunciation so that you know whether children are pronouncing words at the expected level for their age. See page 87 for a picture of how children develop their speech sounds from 18 months old.

Case study: Ahmed, 4 years old
Ahmed pronounces 'yellow' as 'lellow' and 'frog' as 'fwog' He struggles to say longer words such as 'crocodile' and 'orangutan'. He loves making up silly rhymes. Familiar people understand everything that he says and unfamiliar people understand almost all of what Ahmed says.

Ahmed's speech is age appropriate.

Case study: Alice, 3 years 11 months   PART 1
Alice struggles to pronounce the sounds that are produced at the back of the mouth (e.g. k, g). She pronounces 'cat' as 'tat' and 'dog' as 'dod'.

Her mum can usually understand her but the nursery staff and the other children often struggle to understand her.

When people don't understand her, Alice perseveres in trying to make herself understood. At times when she can't get her message across, Alice becomes frustrated.

Alice's speech is delayed for her age.
There is more information about the steps that staff have taken to support Alice with her speech sounds.
See Case study: Alice PART 2, page 83

The adult role

1. Take an active approach

Being able to pronounce words depends strongly on listening skills, social skills and talking. Therefore, helping children with all other areas on the **Communication Climbing Frame** will support their development of speech sounds. The emphasis throughout the book is a physically active approach, so many of the activities outlined in the other sections will promote and develop children's ability to pronounce words clearly. For example, action rhymes are an ideal way to help children hear sounds and join in with rhyming words in a fun and relaxed way.

There is research that links gesture and speech very closely as joint ways of expressing thoughts. Iverson and Thelan (1999). People use gesture as they speak in all languages and there are neurological links between the movements of the body and the mouth. *'The motor cortex controlling muscles in the fingers are even more closely linked with those controlling lips and tongue, so articulation of the hand is linked with articulation of words in the mouth.'* (White,

2015). So, being active, particularly with arm movements, is a stimulus for communicating. Movement sessions can help children with their gestures, and the way they express their thoughts through their bodies.

2. Play and Interact

Model clear speech, by sometimes speaking more slowly than you usually talk. Be aware of your natural way of talking, your pronunciation and accent. You may have to adapt your usual way of speaking to enable young children to understand you more easily.

Have a relaxed atmosphere in your setting, this is essential to promote speech sound development. Children are more likely to have a go experimenting with sounds within words if they feel relaxed and confident in the setting.

Always model positively, if you notice that a child hasn't said a word correctly, respond by modelling that word back to them in a positive way. For example, if a child says

"I like dods" (instead of dogs), simply respond with 'You like dogs...wow...I like dogs too!'

Avoid making children say words correctly, for example, 'say shark' as this can be extremely challenging for children and can reduce their self-esteem or impact on their attitude towards speaking.

Get down to the child's level so that the child can see what you're doing with your mouth.

Have fun using your voices together. Use toy phones, microphones, voice changers etc. These are great ways to give the children confidence at exploring with their own voices.

Sing, sing, sing! Nursery rhymes and children's songs usually contain many rhyming words. Singing simple rhyming songs together can help children to become more aware that words are made up of several sounds.

Use children's books with repetitive sounds, for example, 'Sam's Super Stinky Socks' by Paul Bright; also choose books with rhyming words to develop their sound awareness.

It is important to remember that mastering new speech sounds is a complex process. From time to time you may hear someone refer to a child as a lazy talker, however if a child hasn't yet mastered a certain sound, this is by no means due to laziness. If you're discussing a child's speech in front of the child, remember to always keep this positive! (*Principle 6* – Keep it positive)

3. Create the best environment!

Create an environment in which the children are not afraid to experiment and try new things. Ensure there are quiet places to talk and listen, and places that encourage chatting, like dens, tents, cosy areas etc. See the previous sections for this.

4. Working with parents

Dummies or comforters are a very practical and common part of babies' and young children's lives. They help to calm babies, help with teething and send them to sleep. They are special to children because they remind them of cosy times with their family and serve as a bridge for children between the comfort of their family and the big wide world. They help children deal with stressful situations and they are a major comfort at bedtime. A comforter can be an important part of children's healthy emotional development.

However, prolonged use of dummies, and dummies used for long periods throughout the day, can have an impact on a child's speech. If babies have dummies in their mouths throughout the day, they have little chance to 'babble' and practise responding verbally to adult interactions. If toddlers regularly talk when they have a dummy in their mouth, this can cause them to develop speech sound difficulties. This is because they have to try and speak around the dummy. With a dummy in the mouth, it is not possible to say certain sounds that are made at the front of the mouth (e.g. t, d, l). The habits that children develop as a result of prolonged use of dummies can make their speech very difficult to understand. It is important that parents are aware of the effect of dummies on the development of speech.

Encourage parents to be positive about their child's speech. Suggest good practice, such as getting down to eye level and really listening to them, modelling back correct pronunciation naturally, avoiding saying things like 'say it properly', or finishing their sentences. Good communication between practitioners and parents is vital, and a communication book between home and your setting can be particularly useful. Parents can write down what they have been up to at home. This way it will make it easier for you to chat to children about their lives and understand what they are trying to tell you.

Check with parents whether or not the child's hearing has been assessed. If a child is experiencing speech sound difficulties and hearing has not been checked, recommend that parents refer the child to the audiology service in the area. Glue ear (fluid in the ear) is particularly common in nursery-aged children, and this impacts on the way in which children hear sounds.

5. Support children who are learning EAL

Remember that the speech sound development chart (page 81) is based on children who are learning English as their first language.

For children who are learning EAL, their ability to pronounce speech sounds will not necessarily follow these same patterns. Be aware that different languages have different sounds in them. A child who is learning EAL may have difficulties pronouncing sounds that they do not have in their first language.

For example, many languages including Polish and Danish don't have a 'th' sound that occurs frequently in the English language. Similarly the 'w' sound does not occur in languages such as Swedish and German. In Polish the 'r' sound is rolled unlike in English, and Polish also has 'nasal vowels' which do not exist in the English language.

As with all children, patience and good modelling of sounds is essential to support these children to master speech sounds.

6. Provide extra support for children with difficulties

Due to the increasing numbers of children entering school with speech, language and communication difficulties, particularly in disadvantaged areas, there is a huge strain on the UK's National Health Service (NHS) for Speech and Language Therapy services. As a result, there are often lengthy waiting lists for therapy and the number of sessions with a therapist is often limited. For this reason, it is vital that practitioners in settings have the skills to promote and support speech sound development.

There are a number of reasons why a child might experience speech sound difficulties.

'These include hearing problems, poor muscle control of the tongue, lips, teeth and mouth, cleft palate or learning problems. However, often there is no apparent reason for the problem.' (Mountstephen, 2010)

For many children there is no clear reason why they are finding speech sounds a challenge. Some children simply present as delayed. They will be following the typical patterns of speech development, but at a noticeably slower rate than most children.

Other children have what is referred to as disordered speech. These children are making sound errors that are not seen in typical development.

Children who regularly have coughs, colds and ear infections are at a higher risk of having speech difficulties.

'Children who have suffered hearing loss through repeated ear infections are likely to have missed out in terms of access to listening and interacting effectively.' (Mountstephen, 2010)

Some children who experience difficulties with speech sounds may have verbal dyspraxia. Children with verbal dyspraxia have difficulties coordinating the muscles in their mouth. This neurological condition results in *'difficulty in making and coordinating the precise movements of the speech muscles necessary for clear speech.'* (Mountstephen, 2010)

Some children experience difficulties with speech as a result of having limited phonological awareness. This means that they may struggle to discriminate between sounds such as 'tea' and 'key'.

Children who have difficulties pronouncing sounds can find it difficult to make themselves understood. This can be extremely frustrating for a child at times.

Use the strategies and advice in the 'Play and Interact' section for children who have speech difficulties.

Learn the names of key people in the child's life, siblings, family friends, pets etc. This can help you to understand the child when they are trying to tell you something.

Some children will not be aware that they have speech sound difficulties; other children will be highly aware that they have speech sound difficulties. The way in which you should respond and interact with children with speech sound difficulties will depend on their level of awareness of their difficulties. For example, if you are working with a child who is very aware that others struggle to understand him, you will need to build his confidence through a close relationship, so that he feels secure enough to 'have a go' and continue to speak.

Draw attention to the correct way to say a word by saying it repeatedly in a way that is relevant to what the child has said. For example, if a child struggles to pronounce the 'f' in the word 'fish', you could respond with 'Oh yes, I like that fish! Let's feed the fish. That fish is eating it all.'

Avoid asking the child to repeat words or 'say it properly'. It can have a negative impact on the child's confidence and their willingness to experiment with speech sounds if too much attention is drawn to their speech when they are trying to tell you something. Children need to feel relaxed and confident to try new ways of saying sounds.

When you do understand what the child is saying to you, repeat parts back or rephrase what they have said. This will support their confidence with speaking.

If you really can't understand what the child is saying, don't pretend that you can understand them! Get the child to show you in some other way. Many children are good at making themselves understood in some way through gesture or taking you by the hand. Ask questions to narrow down the options. For young children, if you can't figure out what they are trying to say, it is ok to blame your own ears sometimes!

Case study: Alice, 3 years 11 months   PART 2
Alice has trouble pronouncing many of her speech sounds. Nursery staff find it very hard to understand what Alice is saying, although her key person Angela is more tuned in to what she says. Mum reports that she can understand some of what Alice says, however she often finds her difficult to understand too. She reported that Alice can get very frustrated when she does not understand her at home.

Nursery staff have referred Alice to the local Speech and Language Therapy service with her mum's consent. They are following the advice given by the speech and language therapist. This involves spending 5-10 minutes every day working on her target sound.
Nursery staff are modelling the words that Alice is struggling with in context and in a positive way so that she is hearing the correct way to say them.
There is also another child in Alice's nursery who struggles with speech sounds, so Angela (Alice's key person) will often spend time with the two children together doing activities such as 'clap the beat', 'silly sound books' and singing songs and nursery rhymes.
Everyone is very positive about the efforts both children make when they speak, making sure that they maintain their confidence to talk.

Alice's mum has noticed an improvement in Alice's speech since the nursery staff have been following the speech and language therapist's advice, and she has also been playing games with her. She feels Alice is now getting frustrated less often at home because her family understand her better. At nursery, Alice will often ask to play 'clap the beat' and she is now getting really good at this.

Stammering

There is one box on the communication chain that relates to speaking fluently. The task of speaking fluently comes after most of the processes required in talking.

Everyone 'trips up' when they are talking sometimes and we all hesitate when we talk now and again. It is not uncommon for children aged between 2 and 4 to have some difficulty with fluency. However, people who stammer, have more difficulties than the rest of us with getting their words out fluently.

They will often repeat the first sound in a word, for example, d.d.d.d.daddy, or, repeat whole words, for example, 'and and and and and', 'I I I I I ' or stretch out sounds, for example, mmmmmmummy. Sometimes they may get completely stuck when trying to speak and may not be able to get the words out at all.

If you have any children in your setting who find it difficult to speak fluently, one of the key strategies is to slow down your own speech when talking to that child. As already highlighted, children mirror what they see and hear. So if children hear adults speaking slowly, they are more likely to speak slowly themselves, which will make it easier for them to be fluent.

Another key strategy is to reduce the number of questions that you ask the child and instead make comments. This way, the communication style is more relaxed and the child is not put under pressure to respond. They will respond on their own terms.

If a child does stammer when talking to you, simply give them time to finish and remain calm. It is important that the child can see that you're listening and that there is no rush. With children who stammer, ensure that you praise them and recognise the positives as this will help to maintain their confidence.

Many children go through a short period of dysfluency during the early years. However, some children will continue to stammer throughout their childhood and adult life. If you are worried about a child's ability to get their words out, it is important to have a conversation with the child's parents. The research shows that the earlier a child with a stammer receives Speech and Language Therapy support, the more likely it is that the therapy will be effective (British Stammering Association, 2009). Speech and language therapists support children who stammer in a range of ways, depending on the child's situation.

Some children will not be aware that they stammer; however for some children, stammering can be extremely frustrating. It is important to acknowledge how a child is feeling if their speech is upsetting them and becoming the cause of great frustration. Acknowledge their difficulty gently and positively. A good way to acknowledge the difficulty is to refer to their speech as 'bumpy'. For example, you may say something like 'talking is a bit bumpy today, but that's ok', or 'talking can be a bit tricky sometimes'. Avoid asking children to slow down.

Get active!

Activity 1: Clap the beats! Stamp the beats!

Why? The syllables within a word are the different segments that make up the word when you pronounce them, for example, 'act...ive' has 2 syllables and 'phys..i..cal has 3 syllables. Clapping the syllables helps children to learn how words are made up, eventually helping with reading and also with breaking the word down to pronounce it.

Resources: Toys or pictures (a combination of toys with 1, 2, 3 and 4 syllables), a bag
1 syllable: sheep, tree, chair, bus, beans
2 syllable: chicken, flowers, table, pizza, hedgehog
3: syllable: dinosaur, spaghetti, banana, elephant, hospital
4 syllable: alligator, watermelon, caterpillar, helicopter, ballerina, cauliflower, firefighter.

How?
- Practise clapping some words out together as a group
- The children take it in turns to close their eyes and pick an item (or picture) out of the bag
- The child will probably name the item
- The adult should repeat the name of the item in a loud, clear voice
- The adult should then ask the group 'how many claps?'
- Try to clap out the words (clapping to each syllable).

Helpful hint: Don't actually use the word 'syllable' with the children. Instead, refer to syllables as 'claps' or 'beats'.

MAKE IT MORE ACTIVE! Stand up and clap, stamp or jump instead of clapping. When they have got the hang of it, combine movements, for example, 'DI..NO..SAUR' jump jump clap! Stamp stamp and lift both arms in the air! Use their names too as the words to clap and jump to!

Activity 2: Spot the sound!

Why? This activity helps children to really tune into the sounds at the start of words.

Resources: Two hoops of different colours, a range of items that start with the sound that you have chosen (see below), a range of items that do not start with the sound that you have chosen, a bag or a box big enough for all of the items that you have gathered.
For example, if you have chosen to target the 's' sound first, you could use the following:
Items/toys starting with 's': sock, spoon, snake.
Items/ toys not starting with 's': apple, cup, ball.

How? Place the 2 hoops a short distance away so children can run to them.
Tell the children the sound they need to listen for (d).
Give some examples of words that start with the chosen letter (e.g. door, doughnut).
Explain that one hoop is for sounds that start with the chosen sound (the yes hoop) and the other hoop is for things that start with other sounds (the no hoop).
Let the children pick items out from the bag, ask them to name the item and have a go at running and placing it in the correct hoop.

For example:
'We are going to listen for the sound 'd'.
Lots of things start with the sound 'd'
Door and doughnut both start with 'd'.
[Then pick an item out of the bag]
Does this start with a 'd'?'
Which hoop shall we put it in?

Helpful hint: At the end, ask them to run and fetch an item each and put it back in the bag, saying what each item is.

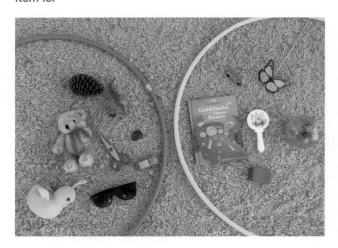

Activity 3: 'I Spy'

Why? 'I Spy' helps children to tune-in to the sounds at the beginning of words. This will give them more awareness of the fact that words contain several different sounds.

Resources: No specific resources are required! You can play this game absolutely anywhere.

How?
- An adult looks around them and chooses an item.
- They then say: 'I spy with my little eye, something beginning with...'
- They should say the sound that the word starts with, for example...something beginning with 'f'!
- The other players then have to look around the room or outside and try to guess what the person has chosen. Encourage them to move around and look in different places.
- When someone guesses correctly, all run to where it is!
- It is then their turn to choose something for everyone to guess.

Helpful hint: For children who are having difficulties guessing the word, give them clues such as, the colour, what it is used for, or where in the room it is. For younger children, get them used to this game by saying, 'I spy with my little eye, a tree!' Or 'a scooter' so they look round to find it, and then choose something themselves.

Activity 4: Silly sound books (4 year olds)

Why? Support the children to make a 'silly sound book'. This will include pictures and drawing of things that begin with a certain sound. This will raise their awareness of sounds in words.

Resources: Magazines, scissors, glue, pencils and crayons, other materials for cutting and sticking, notebooks or scrapbooks.

How?
- Cut out some pictures beforehand of things beginning with that sound, a few per child
- You might actually want to make your own silly sound book beforehand to show the children!
- Explain you are going to be making silly books
- Name the sound they need to think about and explain that their book will have lots of pictures of things starting with that sound
- Let them choose a couple of pictures to stick in their book

from the selection of pictures that you have prepared
- Then encourage them to look through the magazine pages for other things that start with the same sound
- They can also draw their own pictures of things that start with the chosen sound.

Get as silly as you like!

For example, if making a silly sound book for the sound 'p', you could stick in a picture of a pony and then draw a pizza in his mouth! A pony eating a pizza!

Make the most of the fantastic opportunities that this brings to talk with the children about what they have stuck in their silly sound books.

Helpful hint: Some children may have difficulties identifying items that start with a certain sound. If they are not sure what sound a certain words, starts with, make it easier for them by repeating the first sound, for example, 'p..p..pizza!'

Activity 5: Silly words

Why? This helps children really use their mouths to pronounce silly made-up words.

Resources: This could just evolve naturally during any activity, or go alongside making monsters, either drawing or making with dough, recycled materials.

How? Make up names for the monsters such as:
- Solifergophasaurus, Thalikerdocudum, Manominomotty.
- Words can have alliteration too such as: Babaraccabillbo, dippydappydoodah
- All try and say the name of each other's monsters.

Helpful hint: Include some movement by asking them to move like their monster moves.

Get active!

Activity 6: Sound treasure hunt

Why? This is a fun and active way to become more aware of the initial sounds of words.

Resources: Anything that is small and children can easily pick up and carry, for example, play people, cars, animals, bricks, tea set, stones, sticks, leaves, balls.

How?
- Place all the different items around the room or preferably outdoors to make it more active!
- Ask children to find something beginning with...'b', for example ask them for some words that begin with 'b' like 'boat', 'brick', 'bag', 'ball'.

- Let them search for the things, if indoors, they should know where the toys are usually stored
- They run back to you with the thing and tell you what it is as they put it in a box
- At the end of the game, take all the things out of the box and name them. If children bring things that begin with a different sound, say how interesting it is and talk about the sound it begins with
- 'Josh has found a caterpillar! Where did you find it Josh? Let's think what 'caterpillar' begins with...'

Helpful hint: Ask them to take all the things back at the end of the game, or things other children found. For younger children hunt together for the treasure, and emphasise the initial sound.

Activity 7: Rhyme bag

Why? Songs and nursery rhymes are fun, and support children to develop their phonological awareness. Phonological awareness is all about knowing how words are made up, which may impact on a child's ability to say sounds.

Resources: A bag, containing items to represent songs and rhymes for example, a star for 'Twinkle, twinkle, little star', a boat for 'Row, row, row your boat', an egg for Humpty Dumpty, a bag.

How? Place each of the song and rhyme items into the bag.
- Take turns to pull something out of the bag and then all sing the nursery rhyme
- Do big actions with the rhymes, for example, Humpty Dumpty can fall off the wall, then they stand up and gallop for all the king's horses.

Helpful hint: Once the children are familiar with the nursery rhymes, have fun singing in different ways! Try quiet singing, loud, fast, slow!

Activity 8: Arm movement and ribbon sticks

Why? Movement, gesture and speaking are strongly linked, so by using our arms expressively we are stimulating the connections in the brain between the arms, hands and mouth, which helps children to express the spoken word.

Resources: Music of your choice, with a medium to slow beat, ribbon sticks and wavers.

How? Play music and move your ribbon stick around in time to the music, the children will copy and then move to their own rhythm and impulse.
Swirl around, use the ribbon stick high, medium and low, up and down.

Then, put the ribbon sticks down and ask them to use their arms like the ribbon sticks, waving them high and low and swirling around, making the shapes of the ribbons. Ask them to look at their hands, relax their wrists, soften hands and fingers, wave their arms across each other, reach out to the side, up in the air, make big circles.

Demonstrate different movements using one arm then two arms. Enjoy wafting around!

Helpful hint: Lie on your back and do the same with your arms, watching them and following them with your eyes. You can introduce imaginative language, such as 'swirling smoke', 'soft puffy clouds'.

Tables of development

Speech Sounds

Based on children who speak English as their home language.

Approximate age	Speech Sound Development
18-24 months	Children usually use only a limited number of sounds in words, usually including p, b, m, n, w, h. They often miss off the ends of many words at this stage. Children of this age can usually be understood about half of the time with unfamiliar people.
2-3 years	By this age, children use a wider range of speech sounds, usually including p, b, m, n, w, h, t, d, g, k. They often have problems saying the following sounds: 'sh', 'ch', 'th' and 'r', 'w', 'l', 'z'. They will usually shorten longer words, such as saying 'nana' instead of 'banana'. They usually have difficulty pronouncing words that contain consonant clusters (two consonants together) e.g. spider may become 'pider'). They can be understood most of the time by familiar people.
3-4 years	Most children's speech becomes a lot clearer between the age of 3 and 4 years. Many children will have mastered most consonant sounds by four years. They have difficulties with a small number of sounds – for example 'r', 'w', 'l', 'f', 'th', 'sh', 'ch', 'y' and 'z'.
4-5 years	Use most sounds effectively. They may still need to perfect their pronunciation of sounds such as 'ch', 'sh', 'z' and 'th'. They will often have difficulties with longer words such as as 'elephant' or 'spaghetti'.

iCAN website

As a rough guide, people who don't know your child as well as you should be able to understand about 50% of what a child says when they're 2 years old, 90% at age 3, and everything they say by the time they are 3 and a half. (talkingpoint.org.uk)

8-week Development Programme

This programme will embed an active approach to Communication and Language and enrich the overall ethos and learning in your setting. You will focus on a different aspect of provision each week so that you build up a strong communication friendly environment, where interactions between staff and children are fundamental to children's overall well-being and language development.

This 8-week programme can be extended to 10 weeks, if needs be, to accommodate setting events, staff absence etc. However, it is important to maintain the momentum and focus, so that continuous progress and improvements can be made.

8-week Development Programme for under 2s

Week	Adult role	Get active!
Week 1: Focus ACTIVE ATTENTION AND LISTENING **Fostering interests** **Developing relationships** **Improving the environment**	**Read Section 1: Why is it important?** **Get to know** about attention and listening skills. Become familiar with the Leuven scales for well-being and involvement. **Observe** your key children and assess their general levels of well-being and their levels of involvement at different activities. **Read Section 1: The adult role** for guidance on the best environment. **Read Section 1: Get Active!** For active ways to develop attention and listening skills. **Focus on** discovering the interests of your key children and developing open-ended resources.	**Find out** what your key children really like doing. What sparks their interest and grabs their attention. Write this down. **Speak with parents**, find out more about the family and what the children like to do at home. Write this down. **Make special times** for each child, when you play, chat and share books only with them, so that you naturally develop their attention span. **Comment** on children's physical actions with enthusiasm and use words like 'up, down, under, over' when babies and toddlers climb and scramble around equipment. **Improve your resources** like treasure baskets and heuristic play materials where babies and toddlers can explore the properties of things. (See pages 23-24) **Consider the noise levels** in your environment and how individual children respond to noisy times; adapt practice for sensitive children, for example, take them to a quiet area or outdoors to help them feel comfortable. **Share with parents** how screen time and background TV affects children's attention and their ability to listen. **Try 3 new activities** from **Get Active!**
Review	**What worked well?**	**What can you improve? How?**
Week 2 Focus: ACTIVE SOCIAL COM-MUNICATION **You as a role model** **Physical fun!** *Continue* Spending quality time with each child, deepening your relationship	**Read Section 2: Why is it important? and The adult role, Play and interact.** Become more aware of how you **role model** communication to children. Notice your own non-verbal communication and your character traits that influence how you interact with children. **Observe** each other and talk about your different strengths in how you connect and communicate with children. **Discuss** how you complement each other as a staff team. **Become more aware** of your own language with children, how do you get them to cooperate, through instructions or request? Have fun, relax and enjoy their company! **Notice** the non-verbal communication of your key children.	**Make special times** with each child part of everyday practice, tuning in to their interests and preferences. **Play physical and social games** with babies and toddlers, like crawling races, hide and seek, dancing together, playing with balloons and bubbles, action songs, anything to help children enjoy being together in a group. **Play physical games** that involve fun with others, like hide and seek, throwing bean bags. Have fun!
Review	**What worked well?**	**What can you improve? How?**

8-week Development Programme for under 2s

Week	Adult role	Get active!
Week 3 Focus: ACTIVE SOCIAL COMMUNICATION **Developing friendships** **Role play, singing and dancing** *Continue* having fun with children	**Read Section 2: The adult role, Create the best environment** **Consider** your environment in terms of welcome for parents and children, cosy places to relax and chat, enough resources (building bricks, wheeled toys, posting toys etc.) for children to play comfortably together. **Notice** the older toddlers who are beginning to seek out friends. **Notice** and comment when children help each other. **Record** the social skills of your key children in your usual system. Use Early Years Outcomes (2013) PSED Relationships.	**Develop early friendship skills** with babies and toddlers, by having conversations with them on a 1 to 1, listening and responding, playing peek-a-boo. **Make the home role play area more interesting** with, for example playdough, or uncooked pasta for food, or baby baths to wash dolls. **Continue to sing and dance** together. Introduce simple turn-taking like passing a ball to each other **Make this a week where you foster friendship skills** such as playing side by side, singing 'row the boat' holding hands, and encourage older toddlers to play together. **Spend time with shy and quiet toddlers** to help them share a story or play with the garage, water or sand alongside one other child. **Plan activities where older toddlers have to take turns,** such as rolling cars down a ramp, running in and out of cones, jumping off something. Continue to have physical fun; use a parachute, encourage helping each other on the climbing equipment, and when balancing. **Encourage older children to help younger** children if sharing outside play space.
Review	**What worked well?**	**What can you improve? How?**
Week 4 Focus: ACTIVE UNDERSTANDING **Books** **'Action' language** **Singing** *Continue* Good practice from weeks 1, 2 and 3	**Section 3: Why is it important?** Check the receptive language skills of your key children against the table on page 61 **Use Get Active!** For physical activity ideas, try 3 new games. **Learn** a new song.	**Share books** with children on a 1 to 1 or in a small group. When sharing stories, **use props and do physical actions**, for example, pretend to be 'The Hungry caterpillar' munching through the food, and Mr Bear getting up and going to sleep in different places (Peace at Last by Jill Murphy). Notice the involvement and attention that children show. With babies, emphasise the actions in the story by miming and doing them. **Play physical games** telling children to stand on one leg, jump 5 times, go under the blanket, through the tunnel etc. focusing on verbs like stamp, wave, run, dance, twirl and adjectives like high, low, fast, slow. With babies, comment on their movements, like rolling over, crawling, reaching, waving, kicking etc. emphasising the verb and their actions. **Sing songs** spontaneously.
Review	**What worked well?**	**What can you improve? How?**

8-week Development Programme for under 2s

Week	Adult role	Get active!
Week 5 Focus: ACTIVE UNDER-STANDING **Interaction** **Time for reflection** (See page 101) *Continue* Good daily practice	**Read Section 3: The adult role** **Focus** on the way you speak, what you say and how you use gesture. **Consider** a sign support system for use throughout the setting. **Check** that resources are well organised and labelled with words and pictures. Take time to **reflect** on your practice so far. **Observe** your key children, and consider the progress they have made over the last few weeks because of your communication, your relationship with them and following their interests. **Record** anecdotal evidence of children's language and social skills and discuss this as a staff team.	**Slow your speech down** with babies and toddlers when speaking, and notice what happens! Give children time to respond and really listen to them. Be very aware of trying to **develop their understanding** of words. Notice what they understand and what they need help with, and use fewer words and more gestures to help them. **Model language** as they play, such as, it's full, empty, you are rolling, sliding down etc. **Comment more** and ask fewer questions. **Try out some ICW tasks** with your older toddlers to check their levels of understanding. Use this week to focus on your interactions. **Use routines** for deepening your relationship with key children, by interacting specifically with them.
Review	**What worked well?**	**What can you improve? How?**
Week 6 Focus: ACTIVE TALKING **Conversations** **Commenting on actions** **Sustained shared thinking** *Continue* Good daily practice	**Read Section 4: Why is it important?** **Notice** how your babies and 1 year olds communicate and respond; can you understand their sounds and gestures? Make a note of the words they use and the type of vocabulary page 64 **Read Section 4: The adult role** **Check** your key children against the typical language development chart Page 76	**Copy babies sounds** and have fun with your voices! Use animal noises and vehicle sounds. **Talk with children** about what they are doing and seeing. Have conversations! LISTEN to the children more. Play games with your voices. **Notice and comment** on what children do with their bodies, for example, 'you are spinning around with one hand on the floor'. **Develop 'sustained shared thinking'** with your key children by becoming engrossed with them in their play and conversations. This can happen at all ages.
Review	**What worked well?**	**What can you improve? How?**

8-week Development Programme for under 2s

Week	Adult role	Get active!
Week 7 Focus: ACTIVE TALKING Environment Role play Sensory play *Continue* Good daily practice	**Read Section 4: The adult role, Create the best environment.** **Review** your environment and provide 'sociable comfortable places indoors and outdoors'. **Try 3 different multi-sensory activities** and focus on the language!	**Create dens and cosy areas** indoors and outdoors where children are motivated to chat. **Use activities in 'Get Active!'** to encourage children to talk. **Interact** with children in multi-sensory activities, commenting on what they do and using words to describe how it feels. With babies, use jelly, custard, spaghetti as a safe medium to explore.
Review	**What worked well?**	**What can you improve? How?**
Week 8 Focus: ACTIVE SPEECH SOUNDS Action rhymes Model speech	**Read Section 5: Why is it important?** **Check** the table of speech sounds development on page 87 and notice the sounds your key children can and cannot say. Notice how they swap sounds too. **Speak** more slowly to children, model speech clearly. **Learn** 2 new action rhymes – share your rhyme and song repertoire as a team!	**Have fun** with toy phones, karaoke machines, microphones. **Do lots of action rhymes** and singing. **Find books with rhyming words and alliteration**, like: 'Peek-a Who?', by Nina Laden 'Sheep in a Jeep', by Nancy E Shaw 'Cuckoo Can't Find You', by Lorianne Siomades 'Llama, Llama, Red Pyjama', by Anna Dewdney 'Chikka Chikka Boom Boom', by Bill Martin Jr and John Archambault 'Brown Bear, Brown Bear, What Do You See?', by Bill Martin Jr.
Review	**What worked well?**	**What can you improve? How?**

Prime Time **COMMUNICATION AND LANGUAGE**

8-week Development Programme for 2-3s

Week	Adult role	Get active!
Week 1: Focus ACTIVE ATTENTION AND LISTENING **Fostering interests** **Developing relationships** **Improving the environment**	**Read Section 1: Why is it important?** Get to know about attention and listening skills. Become familiar with the Leuven scales for well-being and involvement. Observe your key children and assess their general levels of well-being and their levels of involvement at different activities. **Read Section 1: The adult role** for guidance on the best environment **Read Section 1: Get Active!** For active ways to develop attention and listening skills. **Focus on** discovering the interests of your key children and developing open-ended resources.	**Find out** what your key children really like doing and what sparks their interest and grabs their attention. Write this down. **Speak with parents**, find out more about the family and what the children like to do at home. Write this down. **Make special times** for each child, when you play, chat and share books only with them, so that you naturally develop their attention span. **Comment** on children's physical actions with enthusiasm and use words like 'up, down, under, over' when climbing around equipment. **Consider the noise levels** in your environment and how individual children respond to noisy times; adapt practice for sensitive children, for example, take them to a quiet area or outdoors to help them feel comfortable. **Share with parents** how screen time and background TV affects children's attention and ability to listen. **Try 3 new activities** from **Get Active!** **Review resources** in terms of open-ended learning, where children can choose how to use and play with things. Observe how well and how often children develop their own ideas and create their own challenges. Write this down in your observation system. **Make your group times more interesting** by using puppets, telling stories with props, including more movement and activity. Work on improving your skills, by being relaxed, positive and responsive to children's needs.
Review	**What worked well?**	**What can you improve? How?**
Week 2 Focus: ACTIVE SOCIAL COM-MUNICATION **You as a role model** **Physical fun!** *Continue* Spending quality time with each child, deepening your relationship	**Read Section 2: Why is it important? and The adult role, Play and interact.** Become more aware of how you role model communication to children. Notice your own non-verbal communication and your character traits that influence how you interact with children. **Observe** each other and talk about your different strengths in how you connect and communicate with children. **Discuss** how you complement each other as a staff team. **Become more aware** of your own language with children, how do you get them to cooperate, through instructions or request? Have fun, relax and enjoy their company! **Notice** the non-verbal communication of your key children.	**Make special times** with each child part of everyday practice, tuning in to their interests and preferences. **Play physical and social games** that involve fun with others, like hide and seek, throwing bean bags at a target, circuits with cones and hoops, skittles, races, tag, anything that involves 2 or more children. Have fun!
Review	**What worked well?**	**What can you improve? How?**

8-week Development Programme for 2-3s

Week	Adult role	Get active!
Week 3 Focus: **ACTIVE SOCIAL COMMUNICATION** **Developing friendships** **Role play, singing and dancing** *Continue* having fun with children	**Read Section 2: The adult role, Create the best environment** **Consider** your environment in terms of welcome for parents and children, cosy places to relax and chat, enough popular resources (building bricks, cars, trains, wheeled toys, pushchairs and dolls etc.) for children to play comfortably together. **Notice** who are friends in your room and the children who are quiet and tend to play alone. **Notice** and comment when children help each other and share voluntarily. **Record** the social skills of your key children in your usual system. Use Early Years Outcomes (2013) PSED Relationships.	**Develop friendship skills,** by helping children to play alongside each other, and together. Encourage home role play, with tea parties, taking babies for walks etc. Play with dinosaurs and complete a floor puzzle together etc. Have one to one conversations, listen, show genuine interest, comment and respond. **Make this a week where you foster friendships** and encourage children to play with each other. **Create a different role play area.** Such as a pet shop, a café, a car wash, Doctor's surgery, airport, train or bus station depending on children's experiences. Role model the etiquette for each scenario, such as the greeting, 'Good morning, can I help you?' 'How are you today?' **Make the home role play area more interesting** with, for example playdough, or uncooked pasta for food, or baby baths to wash dolls. **Continue to sing and dance** together. Introduce simple turn-taking like passing a ball to each other **Have physical fun** by collecting lots of balls spread from around the area to put in a box, have fun with the parachute. **Spend time with shy and quiet children** to help them join in an activity they enjoy with one other child. **Plan activities where children have to take turns,** such as rolling cars down a ramp, running in and out of cones, jumping off something. **Encourage older children to help younger** children if sharing outside play space.
Review	**What worked well?**	**What can you improve? How?**
Week 4 Focus: **ACTIVE UNDERSTANDING** **Books** **'Action' language** **Singing** *Continue* Good practice from weeks 1, 2 and 3	**Section 3: Why is it important?** Check the receptive language skills of your key children against the table on page 61 **Use Get Active!** For physical activity ideas, try 3 new games, and 2 movement sessions. Learn a new song.	**Share books** with children on a one to one or in a small group. In story sessions, **use props and do physical actions**, for example, pretend to be 'The Hungry Caterpillar' munching through the food or Mr Bear getting up and going to sleep in different places (Peace at last, by Jill Murphy). Notice the involvement and attention that children show. **Play physical games** telling children to stand on one leg, jump 5 times, go under the blanket, through the tunnel etc. focus on verbs like stamp, dance, walk, wave, shake, wiggle, and adjectives like high, low, fast, slow. Do some exercises to music, saying the movements as you do them. **Lead movement sessions** where they pretend to be animals creeping through the jungle, or fish, dolphins, octopus swimming in the sea. Link these sessions to stories they know. **Sing songs** spontaneously.
Review	**What worked well?**	**What can you improve? How?**

8-week Development Programme for 2-3s

Week	Adult role	Get active!
Week 5 Focus **ACTIVE UNDER-STANDING** **Interaction** **Time for reflection** (See page 101) *Continue* Good daily practice	**Read Section 3: The adult role.** **Focus** on the way you speak, what you say and how you use gesture. **Consider** a sign support system for use throughout the setting. **Check** that resources are well-organised and labelled with words and pictures. **Take time** to reflect on your practice so far. **Observe** your key children, and consider the progress they have made over the last few weeks because of your communication, your relationship with them and following their interests. **Record** anecdotal evidence of children's language and social skills and discuss this as a staff team.	**Slow your speech down** with all children when speaking, and notice what happens! Give children time to respond and really listen to them. Be very aware of trying to develop children's **understanding of words**. Notice what they understand and what they need help with, and use fewer words and more gestures to help them. **Model language** as they play, such as, it's full, empty, you are rolling, sliding down etc. **Comment more** and ask fewer questions. **Try out some ICW tasks** with individual children to check their levels of understanding. Use this week to focus on your interactions. **Use routines** for deepening your relationship with key children, by interacting specifically with them.
Review	**What worked well?**	**What can you improve? How?**
Week 6 Focus: **ACTIVE TALKING** **Conversations** **Commenting on actions** **Sustained shared thinking** *Continue:* Good daily practice	**Read Section 4: Why is it important?** **Notice** how well your children communicate. Make a note of the range of words they use and the type of vocabulary. (See page 64). **Read Section 4: Talking, The adult role** **Check** your key children against the typical language development chart. (See page 76).	**Talk with children** about what they are doing and seeing. Have conversations! LISTEN to children more. Play games with your voices, make up silly rhymes when you are playing, whisper. **Notice and comment** on what children do with their bodies, for example, 'you are spinning around with one hand on the floor'. **Develop 'sustained shared thinking'** with your key children by becoming engrossed with them in their play and conversations. This can happen at all ages.
Review	**What worked well?**	**What can you improve? How?**

8-week Development Programme for 2-3s

Week	Adult role	Get active!
Week 7 Focus: **ACTIVE TALKING** **Environment** **Role play** **Sensory play** *Continue:* Good daily practice	**Read Section 4: The adult role, Create the best environment.** **Review** your environment and provide 'talking places'. **Plan** specific vocabulary for activities and play areas. **Try 3 different multi-sensory activities** and focus on the language!	**Interact** with children in new role play areas to model language for café/shop/garage etc. **Create dens and cosy areas** indoors and outdoors where children are motivated to chat. **Use activities in 'Get Active!'** to encourage children to talk. (e.g. Simon says, Treasure hunt, Fruit tasting, Touchy feely boxes).
Review	**What worked well?**	**What can you improve? How?**
Week 8 Focus: **ACTIVE SPEECH SOUNDS** **Action rhymes** **Model speech**	**Read Section 5: Speech Sounds, Why is it important?** **Check** the table of development on page 87 and notice the sounds your key children can and cannot say. Notice how they swap sounds too. **Speak** more slowly to children, model speech clearly. **Learn** 2 new action rhymes – share your rhyme and song repertoire as a team!	**Have fun** with toy phones, karaoke machines, microphones. **Do lots of action rhymes** and singing. **Try 3 activities** from 'Get Active!' to help with speech sounds. **Find books with alliteration**, like: 'Chikka Chikka Boom Boom', by Bill Martin Jr. and John Archambault 'Some Smug Slug', by Pamela Duncan Edwards 'Pigs in Pajamas', by Maggie Smith 'Many Marvellous Monsters', by Ed Heck.
Review	**What worked well?**	**What can you improve? How?**

8-week Development Programme for 3-5s

Week	Adult role	Get active!
Week 1: Focus ACTIVE ATTENTION AND LISTENING **Fostering interests** **Developing relationships** **Improving the environment** **Improving group times**	**Read Section 1: Why is it important?** Get to know about attention and listening skills. Become familiar with the Leuven scales for well-being and involvement. **Observe** your key children and assess their general levels of well-being and their levels of involvement at different activities. **Read Section 1: The adult role** for guidance on the best environment. **Read Section 1: Get Active!** For active ways to develop attention and listening skills. **Focus on** discovering the interests of your key children and developing open-ended resources.	**Find out** what your key children really like doing and what sparks their interest and grabs their attention. Write this down. **Speak with parents**, find out more about the family and what the children like to do at home. Write this down. **Make special times** for each child, when you play, chat and share books only with them, so that you naturally develop their attention span. **Comment** on children's physical actions with enthusiasm and use words like 'up, down, along, sideways, level, through, under, over' when climbing around equipment. **Consider the noise levels** in your environment and how individual children respond to noisy times; adapt practice for sensitive children, for example, take them to a quiet area or outdoors to help them feel comfortable. **Share with parents** how screen time and background TV affects children's attention and ability to listen. **Try 3 new activities** from **Get Active!** **Review resources** in terms of open-ended learning, where children can choose how to use and play with things. Observe how well and how often children develop their own ideas and create their own challenges. Write this down in your observation system. **Make your group times more interesting** by using puppets, telling stories with props, including more movement and activity. Work on improving your skills, by being relaxed, positive and responsive to children's needs.
Review	**What worked well?**	**What can you improve? How?**
Week 2 Focus: ACTIVE SOCIAL COMMUNICATION **You as a role model** **Physical fun!** **Group times** *Continue* Spending quality time with each child, deepening your relationship	**Read Section 2: Why is it important? and The adult role, Play and interact.** Become more aware of how you role model communication to children. Notice your own non-verbal communication and your character traits that influence how you interact with children. **Observe** each other and talk about your different strengths in how you connect and communicate with children. **Discuss** how you complement each other as a staff team. **Become more aware** of your own language with children, how do you get them to cooperate, through instructions or request? Have fun, relax and enjoy their company! **Notice** the non-verbal communication of your key children.	**Make special times** with each child part of everyday practice, tuning-in to their interests and preferences. **Play physical and social games** that involve fun with others, like hide and seek, What's the time Mr Wolf? Duck, duck, goose, throwing bean bags at a target, circuits with cones and hoops, skittles, races, tag, anything that involves 2 or more children. See 'Get Active' for ideas. Have fun! Continue to develop group times.
Review	**What worked well?**	**What can you improve? How?**

8-week Development Programme for 3-5s

Week	Adult role	Get active!
Week 3 Focus: ACTIVE SOCIAL COMMUNICATION **Developing friendships** **Role play, singing and dancing** **Continue having fun with children**	**Read Section 2: The adult role, Create the best environment.** **Consider** your environment in terms of welcome for parents and children, cosy places to relax and chat, enough popular resources (building bricks, cars, trains, wheeled toys, pushchairs and dolls etc.) for children to play comfortably together. **Notice** who are friends in your room and the children who are quiet and tend to play alone. **Notice** and comment when children help each other and share voluntarily. **Record** the social skills of your key children in your usual system. Use Early Years Outcomes (2013) PSED Relationships.	**Develop friendship skills,** by having one to one conversations, listening, showing a genuine interest, commenting and responding. **Make this a week where you foster friendships** and encourage children to play with each other. **Create a different role play area.** Such as a pet shop, a café, a car wash, Doctor's surgery, airport, train or bus station depending on children's expriences. **Role model** the etiquette for each scenario, such as the greeting, 'Good morning, can I help you?' 'What would you like?' 'How are you today?' **Make the home role play area more interesting** with, for example, playdough, or uncooked pasta for food, or baby baths to wash dolls. **Continue to sing and dance** together. **Have physical fun** with the parachute, playing with balls, races, and jumping through hoops, creating circuits, encourage helping each other on the climbing equipment, and when balancing. **Spend time with shy and quiet children** to help them join in an activity they enjoy with one other child. **Plan activities where children have to take turns,** such as rolling cars or balls down a ramp, running in and out of cones, jumping off something. **Encourage older children to help younger** children if sharing outside play space.
Review	**What worked well?**	**What can you improve? How?**
Week 4 Focus: ACTIVE UNDERSTANDING **Books** **'Action' language** **Singing** *Continue* Good practice from weeks 1, 2 and 3	**Section 3: Why is it important?** Check the receptive language skills of your key children against the table on page 61. **Use Get Active!** For physical activity ideas, try 3 new games, and 2 movement sessions. Learn a new song.	**Share books** with children on a one to one or in a small group. In story sessions, **use props and do physical actions**, for example, pretend to be the Billy Goats trip trapping over the bridge, and the Big Bad Wolf huffing and puffing. Notice the involvement and attention that children show. Put actions into all your storytimes. **Play physical games** to help children understand lots of positional language. For example, ask them to do things like, stand on one leg, jump up high 5 times, turn upside down with their tummies upwards and walk sideways like a crab, try some yoga positions and describe where they put their hands, feet, heads and bottoms, have fun with hoops. See 'Get Active' for ideas. **Dance** to different types of music and focus on moving high, low, fast, slow, sideways, forwards, backwards, smoothly and sharply, marching, floating, twirling. **Do some exercises to music,** saying the movements as you do them. **Lead movement sessions** where they pretend to be animals creeping through the jungle, or fish, dolphins, octopus swimming in the sea. Link these sessions to stories they know. **Sing songs** spontaneously.
Review	**What worked well?**	**What can you improve? How?**

8-week Development Programme for 3-5s

Week	Adult role	Get active!
Week 5 Focus **ACTIVE UNDER-STANDING** **Interaction** **Time for reflection** (See page 101) *Continue* Good daily practice	**Read Section 3: The adult role.** Focus on the way you speak, what you say and how you use gesture. Consider a sign support system for use throughout the setting. Check that resources are well organised and labelled with words and pictures. Take time to reflect on your practice so far. **Observe** your key children, and consider the progress they have made over the last few weeks because of your communication, your relationship with them and following their interests. **Record** anecdotal evidence of children's language and social skills and discuss this as a staff team.	**Slow your speech down** with all children when speaking, and notice what happens! Give children time to respond and really listen to them. Be very aware of trying to develop children's **understanding of words**. Notice what they understand and what they need help with, and use fewer words and more gestures to help them. **Model language** as they play, such as, it's full, empty, you are rolling, sliding down, upside down, swinging etc. **Comment more** and ask fewer questions. **Try out some ICW tasks** with individual children to check their levels of understanding. Use this week to focus on your interactions. **Use routines** for deepening your relationship with key children, by interacting specifically with them.
Review	**What worked well?**	**What can you improve? How?**
Week 6 Focus: **ACTIVE TALKING** **Conversations** **Commenting on actions** **Sustained shared thinking** *Continue* Good daily practice	**Read Section 4: Why is it important?** Notice how well your children communicate. Make a note of the sentences, expressions and range of vocabulary they use. **Read Section 4: The adult role** Check your key children against the typical language development chart. Page 76	**Talk with children** about what they are doing and seeing. Have conversations! LISTEN to children more. Play games with your voices, make up silly rhymes when you are playing, whisper. **Notice and comment** on what children do with their bodies, for example, 'you are spinning around with one hand on the floor'. **Develop 'sustained shared thinking'** with your key children by becoming engrossed with them in their play and conversations.
Review	**What worked well?**	**What can you improve? How?**

8-week Development Programme for 3-5s

Week	Adult role	Get active!
Week 7 Focus: **ACTIVE** **TALKING** **Environment** **Role play** **Sensory play** *Continue:* Good daily practice	**Read Section 4: The adult role, Create the best environment.** Review your environment – provide 'talking places'. **Plan** specific vocabulary for activities and play areas. **Try 3 different multi-sensory activities** and focus on the language!	**Interact** with children in new role play areas to model language for café/shop/garage etc. **Create dens and cosy areas** indoors and outdoors where children are motivated to chat. **Use activities in 'Get Active!'** to encourage children to talk (e.g. Simon says, Treasure hunt, Fruit tasting, Touchy feely boxes).
Review	**What worked well?**	**What can you improve? How?**
Week 8 Focus: **ACTIVE** **SPEECH** **SOUNDS** **Action rhymes** **Model speech**	**Read Section 5: Why is it important?** **Check** the table of speech sounds development on page 87 and notice the sounds your key children can and cannot say. Notice how they swap sounds too. **Speak more slowly** to children, model speech clearly. **Learn** 2 new action rhymes – share your rhyme and song repertoire as a team!	**Have fun** with toy phones, karaoke machines, microphones. **Do lots of action rhymes** and singing. **Find books with alliteration**, like 'Chikka Chikka Boom Boom', by Bill Martin Jr. and John Archambault, 'Dinorella, A prehistoric Fairy Tale', by Pamela Duncan Edwards 'Some Smug Slug', by Pamela Duncan Edwards 'Princess Prunella and the Purple Peanut', by Margaret Atwood 'There's a Wocket in my Pocket', by Dr Seuss 'Princess Pigtoria and the Pea', by Pamela Duncan Edwards 'Pigs in Pajamas', by Maggie Smith **Try 3 activities** from 'Get Active!' to help with speech sounds.
Review	**What worked well?**	**What can you improve? How?**

Week 5 (All ages)

Thinking week!

This is the week where you review practice, look at 'where are we now?' and plan ahead.

As a team, discuss the changes you have made and the new routines and activities you have introduced over the past 5 weeks. Record what has worked well, what you would change, and what you would still like to improve. Research resources and equipment issues.

Your everyday practice and nursery ethos for Communication and Language should now be well-established, with all staff building stronger bonds with children, having more conversations and emphasising language through fun physical activities and active learning.

The key to continued good practice is to constantly **observe** children's play, and find out about their interests and fascinations. Then base your planning for the environment, equipment, activities and interactions on this essential knowledge.

Overall review and future plans

Provision	Changes	What works well Why?	What does not work well, Why?	Improvements, When? Who?
Attention and Listening Fostering interests Developing relationships Improving the environment Improving group times				
Social Communication You as a role model Physical fun! Developing friendships Role play, singing & dancing				
Understanding Books props and actions 'Action' language Singing Developing interaction				
Talking Conversations Commenting on actions Sustained shared thinking Environment Role play Sensory play				
Speech sounds Action rhymes Model speech Alliteration & rhyme books				

What it's all about!

The Prime Time Communication and Language Programme is about the impact on children. Choose 2 children and describe the progress and changes in their development. Be specific and give examples.

		Child, age, obs context
		Attention and Listening What are their passions? What changes have you noticed in the child's levels of involvement & concentration?
		Social Communication How have their friendship skills developed? How have their non-verbal communication skills improved? How has their role play developed?
		Understanding How has their understanding improved through using books or physical activities? How well do they follow instructions?
		Talking and speech sounds How has their talking developed through role play, sensory play, sustained shared thinking, physical activities, and with your interactions?

Audit

Use this audit before and after you do the 8-week programme. This will highlight areas you are already doing well and those that you can develop.

Audit

0-2 years

Make notes of your practice in the relevant box or on the back of the sheet.

Questions	Established	Developing	Not yet in place	Action	Date
ACTIVE ATTENTION & LISTENING					
Children's interests and involvement					
Do you know what really interests each of your key children?					
Do you know the individual preferences of the babies and toddlers for their routine care (nappies, feeding, sleeping, comfort)?					
Do you spend 'special times' alone with each of your key children, to get to know them better and naturally develop their focus and concentration?					
Do you use Leuven's scales for well-being and involvement? Are they helpful?					
Interaction					
Do you plan action rhymes every day, and sing spontaneously throughout the day?					
Do you use puppets, other props and physical activity to capture children's attention?					
Have you made plans to help children who have difficulties with attention and listening?					
Environment					
Do you have heuristic play with treasure baskets for babies? Are these regularly reviewed, and changed?					
Do you have a good range of open-ended resources indoors and outdoors for toddlers to develop their own ideas and challenges?					
How do you manage the noise levels in your setting? Can you take individual children to a quiet place?					

Audit

0-2 years

Questions	Established	Developing	Not yet in place	Action	Date
ACTIVE SOCIAL COMMUNICATION					
Developing Friendship skills					
Do you play physical and social games with babies and toddlers, such as crawling, rolling, chasing and peek-a-boo?					
Do you have regular conversations throughout the day with babies and toddlers?					
Do you dance every day with babies in your arms and toddlers?					
Have you noticed the friendship skills your children show? What are they?					
Do you encourage social interactions during home role-play with older toddlers?					
Do you sing songs in pairs like 'Row, row, row your boat'? 'Seesaw'? and circle songs holding hands?					
Do you plan simple turn taking activities for toddlers?					
Do you spend time with shy and quiet children, helping them to play with others?					
Do you plan activities to do together such as art, construction, dancing, messy play?					
Do you use simple story books about friends for older toddlers?					
Have you made plans to help children who have difficulties with social communication?					

Prime Time **COMMUNICATION AND LANGUAGE**

Audit

0-2 years

Questions	Established	Developing	Not yet in place	Action	Date
Environment					
Do you have cosy social places indoors?					
Do you have cosy social places outdoors?					
Have you added extra resources to your home role-play, such as baths and nappies for dolls?					
ACTIVE UNDERSTANDING					
Interaction					
Do you share books with children every day?					
Do you make your stories active, with props and physical actions?					
Do you comment on the movements of babies and toddlers, such as rolling, turning, kicking etc.?					
Do you play physical games to emphasise language, using verbs like wiggle, jump, kick, stamp etc.?					
Have you tried to slow your speech down with children?					
Do you model language as you play, and comment on both what you and they are doing?					
Are you making more comments than asking questions?					
Have you assessed your key children's understanding of language using ICW tasks?					
Are you using routines to interact as much as you can with your key children?					

Audit

0-2 years

Questions	Established	Developing	Not yet in place	Action	Date
Do you sing spontaneously with children?					
Do you use gesture to help children understand more easily?					
Have you tried a sign support system, using signs like 'nappy', 'milk' and 'all gone' for babies?					
Do you model positive interactions with children when parents are around?					
Have you emphasised with parents the importance of talking with their children?					
For children learning EAL, have you emphasised the importance of the home language?					
Have you made plans to help children who have difficulties understanding language?					
Environment					
Are your resources and storage areas easily accessible and well-labelled with words and pictures?					
Do you use a visual timetable?					
ACTIVE TALKING					
Interaction					
Do you have conversations with your key children every day? (Review your conversations over a day with each child)					
Do you understand the individual ways your key children communicate with you?					

PHOTOCOPIABLE   Prime Time **COMMUNICATION AND LANGUAGE**

Questions	Established	Developing	Not yet in place	Action	Date
How well do you really LISTEN to children?					
Do you play silly games with your voices, and copy the noises babies make?					
Do you develop sustained shared thinking with children, becoming engrossed in their play with them and being totally connected to their thought processes? Give examples.					
Do you model the appropriate language in the new role play areas?					
Do you add to what a young child says to develop their range of language?					
Do you rephrase for them to help them with grammar?					
Practice					
Have you checked your key children's levels of language development for their age?					
Have you made plans to help children who have difficulties talking?					
Environment					
Do children experience a range of environments every day, indoors and outdoors, to stimulate talking about different 'happenings'?					
Do children experience a wide range of interesting and exciting things every day to prompt them to express themselves in different situations?					

Audit

0-2 years

Questions	Established	Developing	Not yet in place	Action	Date
Do you provide a range of sensory play experiences for babies and toddlers, where you can prompt language and expression?					
Have you developed new 'spaces to chat' both indoors and outdoors?					
Have you considered your background noise and reduced it if needs be?					
ACTIVE SPEECH SOUNDS					
Are you aware of how you speak and pronounce words?					
Do you do lots of actions rhymes and singing every day?					
Do you read books with alliteration and rhyming sounds?					
Have you made plans to help children who have difficulties with speech sounds?					
Do you know who to contact should you need outside agency support for a child?					

PHOTOCOPIABLE   Prime Time **COMMUNICATION AND LANGUAGE**

Audit

2-3 years

Make notes of your practice in the relevant box or on the back of this photocopiable sheet.

Questions	Established	Developing	Not yet in place	Action	Date
ACTIVE ATTENTION & LISTENING					
Children's interests and involvement					
Do you know what really interests each of your key children?					
Do you know the children's individual preferences for their toileting, snacks, meals rest and nap time?					
Do you spend 'special times' alone with each of your key children, to get to know them better and naturally develop their focus and concentration?					
Do you use Leuven's scales for well-being and involvement? Are they helpful?					
Interaction					
Do you plan action rhymes every day, and spontaneously throughout the day?					
Do you use puppets, other props and physical activity to capture children's attention and increase involvement at group time?					
Are you relaxed and flexible in your approach to group times, responding easily and positively to children's moods, comments, behaviour and enthusiasm?					
Have you made plans to help children with difficulties with attention and listening?					

Audit

2-3 years

Questions	Established	Developing	Not yet in place	Action	Date
Environment					
Do you have heuristic play where children can play with a range of materials in a variety of ways?					
Do you have a good range of open-ended resources indoors and outdoors for children to develop their own ideas and challenges?					
How do you manage the noise levels in your setting? Can you take individual children to a quiet place?					
ACTIVE SOCIAL COMMUNICATION					
Developing Friendship skills					
Do you play physical and social games in small groups, such as chasing, hide and seek, What time is it Mr Wolf?					
Do you have regular conversations throughout the day with your key children?					
Do you dance every day with children?					
Have you noticed the friendship skills your children show? What are they?					
Do you encourage friendships during role play, physical play and small world play? How?					
Do you plan specific ways to develop friendships? What are they?					

Prime Time **COMMUNICATION AND LANGUAGE**

Audit

2-3 years

Questions	Established	Developing	Not yet in place	Action	Date
Do you sing songs in pairs like 'Row, row, row your boat'? or 'Seesaw'? and circle songs holding hands?					
Do you plan simple turn-taking activities?					
Do you spend time with shy and quiet children, helping them to play with others?					
Do you plan activities to do together, such as art, construction or messy play?					
Do you use books with stories about friends?					
Have you made up and told a story about friends?					
Have you made plans to help children who have difficulties with social communication?					
Environment					
Do you have cosy social places indoors?					
Do you have cosy social places outdoors?					
Do you create a range of role-play scenarios with children?					
Have you added resources to your home role play?					

Audit
2-3 years

Questions	Established	Developing	Not yet in place	Action	Date
ACTIVE UNDERSTANDING					
Interaction					
Do you share books with children every day?					
Do you make your stories active, with props and physical actions?					
Do you play physical games to emphasise language, using verbs like wiggle, jump, kick, stamp etc.?					
Do you lead movement sessions, pretending to be animals and recreating other experiences they have had?					
Do you link movement sessions to stories that they know?					
Do you lead exercises to music, saying the movements as you do them?					
Have you tried to slow your speech down with children?					
Do you model language as you play, and comment on both what you and they are doing?					
Are you making more comments than asking questions?					
Are you using routines to interact as much as you can with your key children?					
Do you sing spontaneously with children?					
Do you use gesture to help children understand more easily?					
Do you model positive interactions with children when parents are around?					

PHOTOCOPIABLE   Prime Time **COMMUNICATION AND LANGUAGE**

Audit

2-3 years

Questions	Established	Developing	Not yet in place	Action	Date
Practice					
Have you introduced a sign support system?					
Have you assessed your key children's understanding of language using ICW tasks?					
Have you emphasised with parents the importance of talking with their children?					
For children learning EAL, have you emphasised the importance of the home language?					
Have you made plans to help children who have difficulties understanding language?					
Environment					
Are your resources and storage areas easily accessible and well-labelled with words and pictures?					
Do you use a visual timetable?					
ACTIVE TALKING					
Interaction					
Do you have conversations with your key children every day? (Review your conversations over a day with each child)					
Do you understand the individual ways your key children communicate with you?					
Have you checked your key children's levels of language development for their age?					
How well do you really LISTEN to children?					
Do you play silly games with your voices?					

Audit

2-3 years

Questions	Established	Developing	Not yet in place	Action	Date
Do you develop sustained shared thinking with children, becoming engrossed in their play with them and being totally connected to their thought processes? Give examples.					
Do you model the appropriate language in the new role play areas?					
Do you add to what a child says to develop their range of language?					
Do you rephrase for them to help them with grammar?					
Have you made plans to help children who have difficulties talking?					
Environment					
Do children experience a range of environments every day, indoors and outdoors, to stimulate talking about different 'happenings'?					
Do children experience a wide range of interesting and exciting things every day to prompt them to express themselves in different situations?					
Do you plan activities specifically to encourage talking and develop vocabulary and understanding?					
Do you provide a range of sensory play for children where you can prompt language and expression?					
Have you developed new 'spaces to chat' both indoors and outdoors?					

PHOTOCOPIABLE   Prime Time **COMMUNICATION AND LANGUAGE**

Audit

2-3 years

Questions	Established	Developing	Not yet in place	Action	Date
Have you considered your background noise and reduced it if needs be?					
Do you have areas and equipment that prompt speaking, such as a stage, story-telling chair, phones, microphones etc.					
ACTIVE SPEECH SOUNDS					
Are you aware of how you speak and pronounce words?					
Do you have fun with voice changers like karaoke machines and microphones?					
Do you do lots of actions rhymes and singing every day?					
Do you read books with alliteration and rhyming sounds?					
Have you made plans to help children who have difficulties with speech sounds?					
Do you know who to contact should you need outside agency support for a child?					

Audit

3-5 years

Make notes of your practice in the relevant box or on the back of this photocopiable sheet.

Questions	Established	Developing	Not yet in place	Action	Date
ACTIVE ATTENTION & LISTENING					
Children's interests and involvement					
Do you know what really interests each of your key children?					
Do you know the children's individual preferences for their toileting, snacks, meals and rest?					
Do you spend 'special times' alone with each of your key children, to get to know them better and naturally develop their focus and concentration?					
Do you use Leuven's scales for well-being and involvement? Are they helpful?					
Interaction					
Do you plan action rhymes every day, and spontaneously throughout the day?					
Do you use puppets, other props and physical activity to capture children's attention and increase involvement at group time?					
Are you relaxed and flexible in your approach to group times, responding easily and positively to children's moods, comments, behaviour and enthusiasm?					
Have you made plans to help children with difficulties with attention and listening?					

PHOTOCOPIABLE Prime Time **COMMUNICATION AND LANGUAGE**

Audit

Questions	Established	Developing	Not yet in place	Action	Date
Environment					
Do you have a good range of open-ended resources indoors and outdoors for children to develop their own ideas and challenges?					
How do you manage the noise levels in your setting? Can you take individual children to a quiet place?					
ACTIVE SOCIAL COMMUNICATION					
Developing Friendship skills					
Do you play physical and social games in small groups, such as chasing, hide and seek, What time is it Mr Wolf?					
Do you have regular conversations throughout the day with your key children?					
Do you dance every day with children?					
Have you noticed the friendship skills your children show? What are they?					
Do you encourage friendships, during role play, physical play and small world play? How?					
Do you plan specific ways to develop friendships? What are they?					
Do you sing songs in pairs like 'Row, row, row your boat'? 'Seesaw'? and circle songs holding hands?					
Do you spend time with shy and quiet children, helping them to play with others?					

Questions	Established	Developing	Not yet in place	Action	Date
Do you plan activities to do together such as art, construction, messy play?					
Do you use books with stories about friends?					
Have you made up and told a story about friends?					
Have you made plans to help children who have difficulties with social communication?					
Environment					
Do you have cosy social places indoors?					
Do you have cosy social places outdoors?					
Do you create a range of role play scenarios with children?					
Have you added resources to your home role play?					
ACTIVE UNDERSTANDING					
Interaction					
Do you share books with children every day?					
Do you make your stories active, with props and physical actions?					
Do you play physical games to emphasise language, using verbs like wiggle, jump, kick, stamp etc.?					

Audit

3-5 years

Questions	Established	Developing	Not yet in place	Action	Date
Do you lead movement sessions, pretending to be animals and recreating other experiences they have had?					
Do you link movement sessions to stories that they know?					
Do you lead exercises to music, saying the movements as you do them?					
Have you tried to slow your speech down with children?					
Do you model language as you play, and comment on both what you and they are doing?					
Are you making more comments than asking questions?					
Are you using routines to interact as much as you can with your key children?					
Do you sing spontaneously with children?					
Do you use gesture to help children understand more easily?					
Do you model positive interactions with children when parents are around?					

Audit

3-5 years

Questions	Established	Developing	Not yet in place	Action	Date
Practice					
Have you assessed your key children's understanding of language using ICW tasks?					
Have you emphasised with parents the importance of talking with their children?					
For children learning EAL, have you emphasised the importance of the home language?					
Have you introduced a sign support system?					
Have you made plans to help children who have difficulties understanding language?					
Environment					
Are your resources and storage areas easily accessible and well-labelled with words and pictures?					
Do you use a visual timetable?					
TALKING					
Interaction					
Do you have conversations with your key children every day? (Review your conversations over a day with each child)					
Do you understand the individual ways your key children communicate with you?					
Have you checked your key children's levels of language development for their age?					

Prime Time **COMMUNICATION AND LANGUAGE**

Audit

3-5 years

Questions	Established	Developing	Not yet in place	Action	Date
How attentively do you LISTEN to children?					
Do you play silly games with your voices?					
Do you develop sustained shared thinking with children, becoming engrossed in their play with them and being totally connected to their thought processes? Give examples.					
Do you model the appropriate language in the new role play areas?					
Do you add to what a child says to develop their range of language?					
Do you rephrase for them to help them with grammar?					
Have you made plans to help children who have difficulties talking?					
Environment					
Do children experience a range of environments every day, indoors and outdoors, to stimulate talking about different 'happenings'?					
Do children experience a wide range of interesting and exciting things every day to prompt them to express themselves in different situations?					
Do you plan activities specifically to encourage talking and develop vocabulary and understanding?					

Audit

3-5 years

Questions	Established	Developing	Not yet in place	Action	Date
Do you provide a range of sensory play experiences for children, where you can prompt language and expression?					
Have you developed new 'spaces to chat' both indoors and outdoors?					
Have you considered your background noise and reduced it if needs be?					
Do you have areas and equipment that prompt speaking, such as a stage, story-telling chair, phones, microphones etc?					
ACTIVE SPEECH SOUNDS					
Are you aware of how you speak and pronounce words?					
Do you have fun with voice changers like karaoke machines and microphones?					
Do you do lots of actions rhymes and singing every day?					
Do you read books with alliteration and rhyming sounds?					
Have you made plans to help children who have difficulties with speech sounds?					
Do you know who to contact should you need outside agency support for a child?					

PHOTOCOPIABLE   Prime Time **COMMUNICATION AND LANGUAGE**

Audit

Manager

Questions	Established	Developing	Not yet in place	Action	Date
Does the Prime Time Communication and Language (C and L) 8-week programme have high priority in your nursery?					
Do you have a notice board for Prime Time C and L?					
Are you familiar with the 8-week Prime Time C and L programme?					
Do you have key members of staff who are responsible for the programme?					
Do you meet at least once a month with key members of staff to monitor progress and support their work?					
Do you allow key members of staff time to develop the 8-week Prime Time C and L programme?					
Do you provide a slot at staff meetings for key members of staff to update other staff and further the 8-week C and L programme?					
Do you monitor how practice for C and L is improving in each room?					
Do you check plans to see how C and L is being carried out?					
Have you purchased any equipment and resources to help develop the programme?					
Do you know what resources and equipment you need to improve practice in each room?					
What are the key strengths in your nursery of the Prime Time C and L programme?					
What are the areas for improvement for the Prime Time C and L programme?					

Resources

Information has been drawn from:

- Akechi, H. Senju, A. Uibo, H. Kikuchi, Y. Hasegawa, T. & Hietanen, J. (2013) *Attention to Eye Contact in the West and East: Autonomic Responses and Evaluative Ratings.* Available at: http://eprints.bbk.ac.uk/6603/1/Akechi2013PONE.pdf (Accessed on 2nd March 2017)

- American Speech-Language-Hearing Association. *Social Communication Disorders in School-Age Children.* Available at: www.asha.org/Practice-Portal/Clinical-Topics/Social-Communication-Disorders-in-School-Age-Children/ (Accessed on 14th May 2017)

- Baumann,C. & Boutellier, R. (2011) *Physical Activity – The Basis of Learning and Creativity.* Available at: *http://conference.pixel-online.net/edu_future/common/download/Paper_pdf/ITL59-* (Accessed on 9th April 2017)

- Blank, J. (2016) *Prime Time Physical: A Movement Approach to Learning and Development.* London: Practical Pre-School Books.

- Blank, J & Mathews, G. (2017) *Prime Time Personal Social and Emotional Development: A Key Person Approach to Learning and Development.* London: Practical Pre-School Books.

- Blythe, S. (2011) *The Genius of Natural Childhood: Secrets of Thriving Children.* Stroud: Hawthorn Press.

- Bowen, C. (1998) *Typical Speech and Language Acquisition in Infants and Young Children.* Available at: www.speech-language-therapy.com/ (Accessed on 10th May 2017)

- Bowen, C. (1998) *Developmental Phonological Disorders.* Melbourne: ACER Press.

- Bowen, C. (2014) *Children's Speech Sound Disorders.* Oxford: Wiley-Blackwell.

- Bray, M. Working with Parents. In Kersner, M. & Wright, J. (2001) *Speech and Language Therapy.* London: Routledge.

- British Stammering Association. (2009) *Every Child's Chance of Fluency.* London: British Stammering Association. Available at: https://www.stammering.org/sites/default/files/eccf_full_report.pdf (Accessed on 19th May 2017)

- Capuzzi, D and Stauffer, M. (2016) *Human Growth and Development Across the Lifespan: Applications for Counselors.* New Jersey: Wiley.

- Cheldelin, L. (1983) *Your Baby's Secret World. Four Phases for Effective Parenting.* Massachusetts: Branden Press.

- Child Development Guide website. *Stages of Play During Child Development* Available at: www.child-development-guide.com/stages-of-play-during-child-development.html

- Cooper, J. Moodley, M. & Reynell, J. (1978) *Helping Language Development.* London: Edward Arnold.

- Crystal, D. (2003) *Cambridge Encyclopedia of the English Language.* Cambridge: Cambridge University Press.

- David, K. & Dickinson, J. (2012) *How Reading Books Fosters Language Development Around the World.* Cairo: Hindawi Publishing Corporation.

- Department for Children, Schools and Families. (2007) *Primary National Strategy: Supporting Children Learning English as an Additional Language.* Norwich: Department for Children, Schools and Families Publications.

- Department for Education. (2013) Early Years Outcomes. DfE. Available at: www.gov.uk/government/publications (Accessed on 2nd April 2017)

- Department for Education. (2017) *Statutory Framework for the Early Years Foundation Stage.* DfE. Available at: www.gov.uk/government/uploads/system/uploads/attachment_data/file/596629/EYFS_STATUTORY_FRAMEWORK_2017.pdf (Accessed on 17th April 2017)

- Dickinson, D. Griffith, J. Golinkoff, R. & Hirsh-Pasek, K. (2012) *How Reading Books Fosters Language Development around the World.* Journal of Child Development Research. Article ID 602807.

- Dukes, C and Smith, M. (2007) *Developing Pre-school Communication and Language.* London: Sage.

- Early Years Matters (2017) *The Importance of Play.* Available at: (http://www.earlyyearsmatters.co.uk/eyfs/a-unique-child/play-learning/) (Accessed on May 15th 2017)

- Elks, L. & McLachlan, H. (2015) *Language Builders for Verbal ASD. Advice and Activities to Support Verbal Children with Autism Spectrum Disorder.* Cornwall: Elklan.

- Evans Schmidt, M. Pempek, T. Kirkorian, H. Lund, A. & Anderson, D. (2008) *The Effects of Background Television on the Toy Play Behavior of Very Young Children.* Massachusetts: University of Massachusetts.

Resources

- Featherstone, S. (2014) *Learning to Learn*. London: Bloomsbury.

- Garforth, S. (2009) *Attention and Listening in the Early Years*. London: Jessica Kingsley Publishers.

- Geddes, H. (2006) *Attachment in the Classroom. The Links Between Children's Early Experience, Emotional Well-being and Performance in School.* UK: Worth Publishing.

- Ginott, H. Available at: www.quotes.net/quote/40429 (Accessed18th November 2016)

- Goldstein, H. Kaczmarek, L. & English, K. (2002) *Promoting Social Communication: Children with Developmental Disabilities from Birth to Adolescence.* Baltimore: Brookes Publishing Company.

- Gross, J. 2013. Time to Talk: Implementing Outstanding Practice in Speech, Language and Communication. Routledge; Abingdon.

- Halliwell, M. (2003) *Supporting Children with Special Educational Needs*. Oxon: David Fulton Publishers.

- Hamer, C. (2012) *NCT Research Overview: Parent-Child Communication is Important From Birth.* London: NTC.

- Harries, J. (2013) *Getting Ready for Phonics: L is for Sheep.* London: Featherstone Education Limited.

- Hartup, W. (1992). *Having Friends, Making Friends and Keeping Friends: Relationships as Educational Contexts*. Illinois: ERIC Clearinghouse on Elementary and Early Childhood Education.

- Hayes, C. (2016) *Language, Literacy and Communication in the Early Years: A Critical Foundation*. Northwich: Critical Publishing.

- High/Scope Educational Research Foundation. (1998) *Adult-Child Interaction. Trainer Materials.* USA: High/Scope Press.

- Hohmann, M & Weikart, D. (1995) *Educating Young Children: Active Learning Practices for Preschool and Child Care Programs*. Michigan: High/Scope Press.

- High/Scope Educational Research Foundation (1998) *Trainer Guides: Adult-Child Interaction*. USA: High/Scope Educational Research Foundation.

- I CAN. *Factsheet: Speech Sounds*. Available at: www.ican.org.uk/~/media/Ican2/What%20We%20Do/Enquiry%20Service/Speech%20Sounds%20factsheet.ashx (Accessed on 14th May 2017)

- I CAN. (2008) *Speech, Language and Communication Needs and Primary School-aged Children.* Available at: www.ican.org.uk/~/media/Ican2/Whats%20the%20Issue/Evidence/6%20Speech%20%20Language%20and%20Communication%20Needs%20and%20Primary%20School%20aged%20Children.ashx (Accessed 2nd March 2017)

- I CAN (2009) *Speech, Language and Communication Needs and the Early Years*. Available at: www.ican.org.uk/~/media/Ican2/Whats%20the%20Issue/Evidence/7%20Speech%20Language%20and%20Communication%20Needs%20and%20the%20Early%20Years.ashx (Accessed on 2nd March 2017)

- I CAN. (2016) *I CAN Impact Report*. Available at: www.ican.org.uk/~/media/Ican2/What%20We%20Do/About%20us/ICAN_ImpactReport_2016.ashx (Accessed on 2nd March 2017)

- iCommunicate Speech and Communication Therapy. *Activities to Develop Early Social Skills*. Available at: www.icommunicatetherapy.com/wp-content/uploads/2012/09/Activities-to-develop-early-Social-Skills (Accessed on 3rd June 2017)

- Iverson, J. & Thelen, E. (1999) Hand, Mouth and Brain. The Dynamic Emergence of Speech and Gesture. Journal of Consciousness Studies, 6. Available at: http://www.ingentaconnect.com/content/imp/jcs/1999/00000006/F0020011/988 (Accessed on: 18th May 2017)

- JABADAO Organisation. (2007) *The Jabadao Approach*. Available at: https://www.jabadao.org/jabadao-approach (Accessed on 21/04/2017)

- Jarman, E. (2006) *The Communication Friendly Spaces Approach*. Available at: http://www.elizabethjarmantraining.co.uk/index.php (Accessed on 9th March 2017)

- Jensen, E. (2005) *Teaching with the Brain in Mind*. Virginia: Association for Supervision and Curriculum Development.

- Johnson, M. & Wintgens, A. (2001) *The Selective Mutism Resource Manual*. London: Speechmark.

- Kersner, M. & Wright, J. (2012) *Speech and Language Therapy: The Decision-Making Process When Working With Children*. Oxon: Routledge.

- Laever, F. (2009) *Improving Quality of Care with Well-Being and Involvement as the Guides*. Flanders: CEGO Leuven University.

Resources

- Lathey, T. & Blake, T. (2013) *Small Talk: Simple Ways to Boost Your Child's Speech and Language Development From Birth.* New York: The Experiment.

- Law, J. Rush, R, School I. & Parsons, S. (2010) *Modelling Developmental Language Difficulties From School Entry into Adulthood.* Journal of Speech, Language and Hearing Research, 52.

- Lee, W . (2013) *A Generation Adrift*. London: The Communication Trust.

- Levey, S. & Polirstok, S. (2011) *Language Development: Understanding Language Diversity in the Classroom*. London: Sage.

- Lindon, J. (2012) *What Does it Mean to be Three? A Practical Guide to Child Development in the Early Years Foundation Stage*. London: Practical Pre-School Books.

- Lovatt, P. in Haliwell, R (2016) *The Telegraph Lifestyle 'Why Dancing Feels so Good'.* Available at: http://www.telegraph.co.uk/good-news/seven-seas/why-dancing-feels-good/ (Accessed on 15th May 2017)

- Madhani (1994) in Buckley, B (2003) *Children's Communication Skills: From Birth to Five*. Oxon: Routledge.

- Martin, D. (2000) Teaching Children with Speech and Language Difficulties. London: David Fulton Publishers.

- Maude, P. (2010) *Physical Literacy and the Young Child*. In Whitehead, M. (2010) *Physical Literacy Throughout the Lifecourse.* London: Routledge.

- McHolm, A. Cunningham, E. & Vanier, M. (2005) *Helping your child with Selective Mutism.* Oakland: New Harbinger Publications.

- McMinn, J. (2006) *Supporting Children with Speech and Language Impairment and Associated Difficulties.* London: Continuum.

- Mendler, A. (2009) *What Do I Do When? How to Achieve Discipline with Dignity in the Classroom*. Indiana: Solution Tree Press.

- Magic Daycare Nurseries. *The Leuven Well-Being and Involvement Scales.* Available at: http://www.magicnursery.co.uk/pdf_documents/LevelsofWellBeing.pdf (Accessed on 9th May 2017)

- Mistry, M & Sood, K. (2015) *English as an Additional Language in the Early Years: Linking Theory to Practice.* Abingdon: Routledge.

- Mitchell, D. (2014) *What Really Works in Special and Inclusive Education: Using Evidence-based Teaching Strategies.* Oxon: Routledge.

- Mooney, C. (2005) *Use Your Words: How Teacher Talk Helps Children Learn*. St. Paul: Redleaf Press.

- Mountstephen, M. (2010) *Meeting Special Needs: A Practical Guide to Support Children with Speech, Language and Communication Needs*. London: Practical Pre-School Books.

- Nash, M. Lowe, J. & Leah, D. (2013) *Supporting Early Language Development: Spirals for Babies and Toddlers.* Oxon: Routledge.

- National Literacy Trust (2010) *10 Reasons Why Play is Important*. Available at: www.literacytrust.org.uk/talk_to_your_baby/news/2332_10_reasons_why_play_is_important (Accessed on 27th March 2017)

- Oxford Dictionary of English (2006) Oxford: Oxford University Press.

- Oxfordshire County Council. (2008) My Space. Creating Enabling Environments for Young Children. Available at: www.oxfordshire.gov.uk/cms/sites/default/files/folders/documents/childreneducationandfamilies/informationforchildcareproviders/Toolkit/My_Space_Creating_enabling_environments_for_young_children.pdf (Accessed on 21st May 2017)

- Ofcom. (2016) *Children and Parents: Media Use and Attitudes Report 2016*. Available at: www.ofcom.org.uk/research-and-data/media-literacy-research/childrens/children-parents-nov16 (Accessed 10th March 2017)

- Panksepp, J. (1998) *Affective Neuroscience: The Foundations of Human and Animal Emotions*. Oxford: Oxford University Press.

- Parlakian, R. & Lerner, C. (2010) *Beyond Twinkle Twinkle: Using Music with Infant and Toddlers*. Available at: www.naeyc.org/files/yc/file/201003/ParlakianWeb0310.pdf (Accessed on 2nd March 2017)

- Pepper, J. & Weitzman, E. (2004) *It Takes Two to Talk. The Hanen Program.* Ontario: A Hanen Centre Publication.

- Ray, D.C. (2016) *A Therapist's Guide to Child Development: The Extraordinarily Normal Years*. New York: Routledge.

- Renukadevi, D. (2014) *The Role of Listening in Language Acquisition; the Challenges & Strategies in Teaching Listening.* Tamilnadu: Research India Publications.

Resources

- Reynell, J. (1980) *Language Development and Assessment*. Netherlands: Springer Science.

- Roberts, A. Featherstone, S. (2002) *The Little Book of Treasure Baskets*. Featherstone Education

- Robinson, M. (2011) *Understanding Behaviour and Development in Early Childhood. A Guide to Theory and Practice*. UK: Routledge.

- Roopnarine, J. (2010) *Cultural Variations in Beliefs about Play, Parent-Child Play, and Children's Play: Meaning for Childhood Development.* In Pellegrini, A. (2011) *The Oxford Handbook of the Development of Play.* Oxford: Oxford University Press.

- Rowe, M., (2012) *A Longitudinal Investigation of the Role of Quantity and Quality of Child-Directed Speech in Vocabulary Development*. Journal of Child Development, 83.

- Royal College of Speech and Language Therapists. (2012) Better Communication: Shaping speech, language and communication services for children and young people. Available at: https://www.rcslt.org/speech_and_language_therapy/commissioning/better_communication (Accessed on 14th January 2017)

- Sargent, M. (2016) *100 Ideas for Early Years Practitioners: Supporting EAL Learners*. London: Bloomsbury.

- Scarlett, W.J. Naudeau, S. Salonuis-Pasternak, D. & Ponte, I. (2005) *Children's Play*. London: Sage Publications.

- Sheridan, M. (2008) *From Birth to Five Years*. New York: Routledge.

- Signalong. (2010) *Basic Vocabulary Phase 1*. Kent: The Signalong Group.

- Simpkins, C. & Simpkins, A. (2013) *Neuroscience for Clinicians: Evidence, Models and Practice.* New York: Springer.

- Siraj-Blatchford, I. & Manni, L. (2004) Good Question. Available at: www.nurseryworld.co.uk/nursery-world/news/1100998/question (Accessed on 9th May 2017)

- Spooner, L. & Woodcock, J. (2013) *Teaching Children to Listen: A practical approach to developing children's listening skills.* London: Featherstone.

- Sussman, F. (2016) *A Closer Look at Social Communication Skills of Children with Autism Spectrum Disorder.* Available at: www.hanen.org/helpful-info/articles/a-closer-look-at-social-communication-difficulties.aspx (Accessed on 5th April 2017)

- Sylva, K. Melhuish, E. Sammons, P. Siraj-Blatchford, I. & Taggart, B. (2004) *The Effective Provision of Pre-School Education (EPPE) Project*. Nottingham: DfES Publications.

- Tassoni , P. (2008) Language and Learning From Birth to Three. Early Years Educator Magazine, Volume 10.

- The Communication Trust. (2011) *All Together Now*. Available at: www.thecommunicationtrust.org.uk/media/311/all_together_now_v_2.pdf (Accessed 14th May 2017)

- The National Autistic Society. What is Autism? Available at: www.autism.org.uk/about/what-is.aspx (Accessed on 2nd May 2017)

- The National Literacy Trust. (2009) *Press Information*. Available at: www.thecommunicationtrust.org.uk/media/2111/national_campaign_launch_release_-_for_9th_march.pdf (Accessed on 14th May 2017)

- Weitzmann E. & Greenberg, J. (2008) *Learning Language and Loving it.* Toronto: The Hanen Centre.

- White, J. (2015) *Every Child a Mover.* London: British Association for Early Childhood Education.

- Wing, L. & Gould, J. (1979) *Severe Impairments of Social Interaction and Associated Abnormalities in Children: Epidemiology and Classification.* Journal of Autism and Developmental Disorders, 9.

- Ward, A. (2004) *Attention: A Neuropsychological Approach.* East Sussex: Psychology Press.

- Wasik, B. & Bond, M. (2001) *Beyond the Pages of a Book: Interactive Book Reading and Language Development in Preschool Classrooms*. Maryland: American Psychological Association.

- Watkinson, A. (2009) *The Essential Guide for Experienced Teaching Assistants*. Oxon: Routledge.

- Yule, W. & Rutter, M. (1987) *Language Development and Disorders.* London: Mac Keith Press.

Acknowledgements

We are extremely grateful to the children, staff, parents and especially the managers of the following settings and schools for their determined effort to provide us with a wealth of wonderful images for the book.

- Beaudesert Toddle and Tumble, Cannock Wood, Staffs

- Cradley Play Day Nursery, Halesowen, West Midlands and manager Ann Richards

- Daisy Chain Nursery, Stourbridge, West Midlands and manager Ketrina Hill

- Rabbsfarm Primary School, West Drayton, Hillingdon

Jo would like to say thank you to families Blank and Thornton for the photos of your lovely children and a big thank you to Alan Blank for cooking all the meals!

Alice would like to thank everyone at Rabbsfarm for their amazing support, in particular the nursery staff for being so patient and flexible during the photo shoots. A big thank you to my parents Angela and John Bevan for their constant encouragement and to my partner Dan who couldn't be more supportive.